I0176787

The MYSTERY FANcier

Volume 5 Number 4
July/August 1981

THE MYSTERY FANCIER

Volume 5 Number 4
July/August, 1981

TABLE OF CONTENTS

The MYSTERY FANcier
(USPS:428-590)
is edited and published bi-monthly by Guy M. Townsend,
29 S. Church Street, West Chester, Pennsylvania 19380.
Contributions of all descriptions are welcomed.

SUBSCRIPTION RATES: Domestic second class mail, $12.00 per year (6 is-
sues); overseas surface mail, $12.00; overseas airmail, $15.00. Overseas subscribers please pay in international money order, check drawn
on U.S. bank, or currency; no checks drawn of foreign banks, please.

Second class postage paid at West Chester, Pennsylvania.

Copyright 1981 by Guy M. Townsend
All rights reserved for contributors
ISSN:0146-3160

WILDSIDE PRESS

Mysteriously Speaking ...

Well, it's July--or it will be when I get this issue to the post office--and TMF is right on schedule. Except for a few reviews, everything I had on hand appears in this issue, so get those articles, letters, and reviews to me, folks, or we may fall behind again for want of enough material.

I've taken advantage of (or, some might say, abused) my editorial position to slip several pages of books for sale into the middle of this issue. These things are breeding like coathangers in a dark closet, so help save me from being over-run by them by buying a couple of armloads from me. Every penny I make will go toward paying for the overhaul of my great-great-aunt Tillie's dialysis machine (or some other equally worthy cause--trust me).

Two new items deserve mention, the first being a special issue of Iwan Hedman's DAST. For years now, Iwan and I have had a swap arrangement--I send him TMF, he sends me DAST, and no money changes hands. For the most part, I have been more tantalized than edified by the arrangement. Iwan reads English, but I certainly don't read Swedish, and, aside from an occasional article or letter in English, most of DAST's contents has remained a mystery to me. But my patience has at last been rewarded, for in this special issue are found articles on about twenty Scandinavian mystery writers--*and the entire issue is in English!* If you have the slightest interest in what is going on in the mystery field in Scandinavia, this issue is indispensable. Write to Iwan (that's Iwan Hedman, Flodins väg 5, S152 00 Strängnäs, Sweden) and beg him to sell you a copy. I haven't the faintest idea how much the issue costs, or even if Iwan is making it available to anyone other than subscribers, but if pleading doesn't work you might try threatening him with grievous bodily harm--believe me, this issue is worth a few nights in the slammer.

John D. MacDonald fans take note. Copies of Jean and Walter Shine's *Bibliography of the Published Works of John D. MacDonald, with Selected Biographical Materials and Critical Essays* are still available from The Patrons of the University of Florida Libraries (to whom you should make out your check for $9.00), 217 Library West, University of Florida, Gainesville, FL 32611. Walter sent me photostats of the title page and the table of contents (but, alas, no review copy); it's 8½"x11", plastic-spiral bound, and it's 236 pages long.

1

PETERMAN FROM THE OLD SCHOOL
BY ROBERT SAMPSON

The pulp detective fiction magazines of the 1920's con-
tained about as many crook stories, by weight, as stories of
mystery and detection. The first magazine fully dedicated to
this fiction, *Street and Smith Detective Story Magazine,* loaded
its weekly pages with the crook story and poured forth a romantic stream of crime emperors, thugs, pick-pockets, and nice
young heroes who enjoyed breaking the law for justice.

Some criminal characters perished in one issue. Others,
for reasons obscure to modern eyes, moved into their own series,
appearing in chains of stories, years long.

One of these long-lived characters was a lanky, long,
loose-jointed old scoundrell who had been "a peterman, a penny
weighter, scratch man, steerer, pratt digger, gorilla, slough
worker, notch cutter, and booze runner." "Hair well streaked
with gray," says the police report. "Large and prominent nose,
with coarse pores, gray eyes, several gold teeth. Six feet
high."

The report goes on to add that he is a graduate of various
institutions, including "Sleepy Holler, the Copper John,
Charlie Adams, the Pork Dump at Clinton, and some more."

"These comprise the credentials of Big-Nose Charlie, that
engaging fellow whose career extended from 1917 to 1934 in the
S&S Detective Story Magazine and *Best Detective Magazine*--the
latter reprinting material from the former. The series was
written by Charles W. Tyler, a newspaper man whose work filled
Railroad Stories and *Detective Story Magazine* during the 'teens
and 'twenties. Not all the Big-Nose Charlie stories have been
tabulated, but it's estimated that between fifty and seventy-
five were published. More, maybe. Charlie is an engaging fellow, and readers gobbled his adventures.

He is formerly of Kerry Village, Boston. You might tell
it in his speech--a peculiar patois that is part transcription
from the American, part 1917 thug talk, both parts well stewed
in a vaudville-based Boston accent. Thus:

Yuh look forrard t'keep fr'm lammin' int' trouble, but yuh flicker
yuh glim behint so's trouble won't run yuh down.

At times his manner can be formal, or even courtly:

If yuh will puddin' meh f'r bein' so bold.

At other times he is vaporously vague:

DETECTIVE: "Wad you doin' in Florida?"
CHARLIE: "Oh, I wuz j'st lookin' around." Big-Nose Charlie indi-
cated the world at large with an airy, little movement of his hand.
He then cocked an eye at a cloud that hung low on the eastern sky.
"Ut looks like rain," he suggested amicably.

The police look upon him coolly. "Watch out for that dumb-
looking old goat who's dressed up like a birthday cake," they
warn. They always warn too late. That dumb-looking old goat
strikes fast, with a grand mixture of sly indirection and
direct assault.

His crimes are simple as a line between two points. Only his amazing gyrations before and after the event are dazzling. If his hauls are relatively small--he thinks no higher than $2,000 to $3,000--still his gall is immense.

To demonstrate: "Big-Nose Charlie at the Policeman's Ball" (April 16, 1921: *Detective Story Magazine*). An evil jeweler has substituted glass for the diamond in Charlie's ring. Much annoyed, Charlie marches back to the shop. There he whacks the jeweler firmly, robs him, exits. After that, while the police whiz about on his trail, he attends the policeman's ball and dances with the commissioner's wife. When the first hue and cry dies down, he steps grandly off into the night.

Very direct action. It is characteristic.

Arriving in Palm Springs, Florida, he finds himself regarded by Detective J.B. Firebolt. To keep Firebolt occupied, Charlie hires a beach bum to wear his clothing. He, himself, slips off to a hotel where a real estate swindler is displaying a roll of $2,000.

This roll Charlie secures in the simplest possible way. He grabs the wallet and leaves. Firebolt never sees him going.

Like most old-line crooks, Charlie has police officers glowering after him in every city. Up in Boston, Inspectors Borsey and Morrison give thanks that the "old shyster" is not around. In Los Angeles, Detectives South and Cornell deplore his presence.

It is Inspector Morrison, however, who runs across Charlie in El Paso. Our hero stands grandly in a Mexican bar, where he has met Mr. Arbielhide of Boston. Mr. A. has a pocket fat with cash. He has been using the mails to defraud.

As usual, Charlie is direct. He lures Mr. A. to a taxi, whops him over the head, pulls the hat down over his eyes, and departs. Mr. A.'s howls, upon awaking, attract Morrison, who is in town to pick up a prisoner, and his host, an El Paso detective.

All together, they cross the river into Mexico to fetch Charlie back. Which is illegal, sure enough. But Charlie has greased the palms of everybody at the jail and everybody lounging around outside it. The U.S. police get arrested. Charlie, smiling gently, glides out the back door, a respected friend of Mexico. ("Big-Nose Charlie's Ha-Ha," January 10, 1931.)

From Mexico he moves to Los Angeles ("Big-Nose Charlie, Racketeer," August 15, 1931). Once there, he talks himself into the presence of an L.A. gangster and robs him, in his own car, of $7,000. This time he escapes through the studied indifference of some police officers. They are not overly fond of politically connected gangsters.

Charlie's technique never loses its direct freshness. Hundreds of warrants must have waited for him. In February 13, 1932 (still *Detective Story Magazine*), he returns to Boston. "Big-Nose Charlie's Safe" tells how he lured away a diamond merchant and tied him up in a hotel room. (All the while, Inspector Morrison haunts Charlie's every move.) Charlie then arranges for the jeweler's safe to be moved out of his office. While this is being done, Charlie feeds peanuts to a squirrel. When the safe is delivered to its new address, he cleans it out and vanishes. The whole thing occupies one restful afternoon.

Well, yes, you're right. But these are comic stories, you see. Not heavy on grim reality, but charming, insubstantial.

The stories bubble and froth with light-headed foolery, like very light wine, highly carbonated.

That comic touch explains how Charlie can commit his modest crimes through the years and still please readers. His victims are all unpleasant--mainly crooks themselves. You don't mind seeing a crook get stung, do you? You don't mind seeing the police bump into things and fall down? Of course not.

That's the way it was in *Detective Story Magazine*--crook diddles crook and the police bobble around, and so the years slip by. There have been worse formulas.

HUMOR, HORROR, AND INTELLECT
GILES MONT OF RUTH RENDELL'S A JUDGEMENT IN STONE

By Jane S. Bakerman

In 1977 Ruth Rendell published her seventeenth crime novel, *A Judgement in Stone* (London: Hutchinson, 1977, Garden City, N.Y.: Doubleday, 1978; citations refer to Doubleday edition), one of the best fictions of that year. An inverted mystery, *Judgement* recounts the last few months in the lives of a Suffolk family, George and Jacqueline Coverdale and two of their children: Melinda, George's daughter, and Giles Mont, Jacqueline's son, both children of the couple's earlier marriages. The murder is announced in the first sentence of the book, and the interest and tension spring from the reader's keenly whetted curiosity about the details of the crime itself, from the very genuine motivations Rendell depicts, and from the appeal of the victims, all pleasant, likable, if imperfect, people.

The motivations of Eunice Parchman, one of the pair of killers and the Coverdales' maid, arise from her illiteracy and her growing fear and hatred of the very literate and somewhat manipulative Coverdales (Jane S. Bakerman, "The Writer's Probe: Ruth Rendell as Social Critic, *The MYSTERY FANcier* 3, no. 5 [September/October 1979]: 3-6). The motivations of the second murderer, Joan Smith, a religious fanatic who becomes totally unbalanced in the course of the story, are also vital to the plot; symptoms of Joan's madness are *her* growing hatred of the Coverdale family, her conviction that she is God's avenger toward them, and her manic loyalty to her friend, Eunice Parchman. Rendell generates enormous interest in the development of these two unappealing women, an interest steadily fed by a very clever authorial device.

Both Eunice and Joan are not only compelling characterizations in their own rights, but they are also steadily underscored, as it were, by being compared to one of the book's other key characters, Giles Mont, a seventeen-year-old who, "like all true eccentrics, . . . thought other people very odd" (p. 19). Giles *is* odd; he is also a very real and a very appealing character, and, like the other members of his family slaughtered by Eunice and Joan, his is a realistically drawn figure, full of human faults but also full of decency and therefore very attractive. Giles functions in this novel in several ways. His cerebral, ever modifying "love affair" with Melinda, his stepfather's daughter, lends interest and humor, revealing the boy for the child which in some ways he remains. Also, Giles' preoccupation with his studies and with his intense reading program allows for stark contrast with Eunice Parchman's illiteracy. And, very importantly here, his own fascination with religion and his hectic, sometimes amusing but apparently serious quest not only contrasts him with the shallow, wild Joan Smith, but also allows Rendell to explore one of her favorite interests, theology (another Rendell novel, *Murder Being Once Done* [1972], explores the impact of another religious cult upon the child of two of the believers); further, Giles, Joan, and their startlingly different searches for faith permit their creator to explore the novel's second theme, the effects of their faiths on their personalities. Rendell, herself, has commented on these interests:

> I *try* to have, often, not always, a theme as well as a plot. I'm
> quite interested in patterns and formalism and working the thing
> out, and I am also very interested in obscure religious sects....
> I'm very interested in theology; I read a lot of theology--I have
> no religion, but I like theology; it's good; it amuses me and
> entertains me very much. (Unpublished interview notes, Summer,
> 1977.)

Because she handles her intent and her interest so well, Rendell causes them both to interest her readers, and the major tool for generating that interest in *A Judgement in Stone* is the dreamy, withdrawn, lovable Giles Mont.

Giles is never idealized: "He was over six feet and still growing. His face was horrible with acne, and the day after he washed it his hair was again wet with grease" (p. 17). The characterization of Giles which combines realism, attractiveness, and--very importantly--humor, is one of Rendell's chief means of lightening the tone, for keeping the reader interested and forbearing in the face of the coming horror.

Like most teenagers, Giles is preoccupied with love and sex, and his romanticizing, which focuses on his stepsister, Melinda, is colored by his devotion to reading:

> On the surface, his relationship with her was casual and even
> distant, but in Giles' heart, where he often saw himself as a Poe
> or Byron, it simmered as incestuous passion. This had come into
> being or been pushed into being by Giles six months before. Un-
> til then Melinda had merely been a kind of quasi-sister. He knew,
> of course, that since she was not his sister or even his half-
> sister there was nothing at all to stop their falling in love
> with each other and eventually marrying. . . . But this was not
> what Giles wanted or what he saw in his fantasies. In them he
> and Melinda were Byron and Augusa Leigh who confessed their
> mutual passion while walking in Wuthering Heights weather on the
> Greeving Hills, a pastime which nothing would have induced Giles
> to undertake in reality. There was little of reality in any of
> this. In his fantasies Melinda even looked different, paler,
> thinner, rather phthistic, very much of another world. Confront-
> ing each other, breathless in the windswept darkness, they spoke
> of how their love must remain forever secret, never of course to
> be consumated. And though they married other people, their pas-
> sion endured and was whispered of as something profound and in-
> definable. (p. 18)

Also like most other teenagers, Giles is selfish; preoccupied with his own interests, he tends to neglect his family. Sometimes he seems to his mother, Jacqueline, "rather like ... a harmless resident ghost. . . . It stalked the place, but it didn't bother you or damage things, and on the whole it kept quietly to the confines of the ahunted room" (p. 129). He is not, however, totally unmindful of his mother: "Occasionally it flashed across Giles' brain that he ought, say once a day, to utter a whole sentence rather than a monosyllable to his mother. He was quite fond of her really. So he forced himself" (p. 98). He needs time to be alone to study and to think, and he loves the solitude:

"Some people like being alone." He looked vaguely around his
room, at the heap of clothes, the muddle of books and diction-
aries, the stacks of half-finished essays. . . . He loved it.
It was better than anywhere else except possibly the London
library, where he had once been taken by a scholarly relative.
But they wouldn't let you rent a room in the London library, or
Giles would have been at the top of their housing list. (p. 43)

In search of learning, solitude, and faith, Giles reads
all the time, even, to his mother's despair, at the table.
Posted on the bulletin board in his room is "a text . . . a
line that might have been written for him: *Some say life is
the thing, but I prefer reading*" (p. 74). His mother and
stepfather distrust this obsession a bit, for they fear that
Giles is too much alone; they want him to be "normal" and
"well adjusted"; they don't want him to become too much of an
outsider, even though they are vastly proud of the fact that
his success at school is so great that he's won national attention. The danger that Giles will lose touch with humanity
and reality is important to the book, for losing touch is the
key factor that affects his murderers. And Rendell takes care
to show that Giles does *not* become totally disaffected, that
he moves closer to "reality" as ordinary adults understand it.
She does so by demonstrating that to Giles, abstracted as he
is, other people are also important. He loves Melinda and his
mother, and of course these emotions are a part of his human-
izing process, but he also clearly shows care and concern for
George, his stepfather, whose values are alien to Giles and
whose way of life is unappealing to the lad.

Once, when George is terribly worried about his older
daughter, Giles' other stepsister, who is experiencing a very
difficult childbirth, "Giles made one small concession to the
seriousness of the occasion and the anxiety of the others. He
stopped reading and stared instead into space. Afterward,
when the suspense was over, Jacqueline said laughingly to her
husband that such a gesture from Giles was comparable to a pep
talk and a bottle of brandy from anyone else" (p. 40). And
late in the story, when George is facing a painful social
moment and the family scoffs at the idea that Giles, who will
be present, will be any help,

Giles looked up seriously from his duck and green peas. Something
moved him. His conversion? The fact that it was George's birthday? Whatever it was, he was inspired for once to say the perfect
thing.
"I will never desert Mr. Micawber."
"Thank you, Giles," said George quietly. There was an odd
little silence in which, without speaking or glancing at each
other, Giles and his stepfather approached a closeness never before attained. Given time, they might have become friends. (p. 141)

It is important that Giles' growing tolerance for George
probably stems from a newly found faith as well as from the in-
sights into humanity that he has learned from his books. Joan
Smith, his foil, is quite different; she is a selfish, self-
righteous religious fanatic whose concern even for her friend
and fellow-murderer, Eunice Parchman, stems from self-interest.
After a vicious and licentious early life, Joan has, almost
accidentally, impulsively become a member of the Epiphany

People, a group who stress public confession, witnessing, and
proselitizing:

> On the whole, they were and are a jolly lot. They sing and laugh
> and enter with gusto into their own confessions and those of new
> converts. They talk of God as if He were a trendy headmaster who
> likes the senior boys to call Him by His Christian name. Their
> hymns are not unlike pop songs and their tracts are lively with
> comic strips. The idea of the elect being Wise Men who follow a
> star is not a bad one. The . . . cult would probably have been
> latched onto by young people of the Jesus freak kind but for its
> two insuperable drawbacks distasteful to anyone under forty--and
> to most people over forty, come to that. One is its total embargo
> on sexual activity, whether the parties are married or not; the
> other its emphasis on vengeance against the infidel, which means
> any non-Epiphany Person, a vengeance that is not necessarily left
> to God but may be carried out by the chosen as his instruments.
> In practice, of course, the bretheren do not go about beating up
> their heretical neighbours, but the general impression is that if
> they do they will be praised rather than censured. After all, if
> God is their headmaster, they are all prefects. (p. 91)

For Joan, the allure of the cult is its drama; she can now exploit the sins of her youth, for to her and to many of her
fellow believers, her sensational--and constant--recitals of
the lowness of her past contrasts sharply with what she considers the elevation of her present life and enable her to
occupy the spotlight.

> At first it seems a mystery why all this should have made an ap-
> peal to Joan. But she had always loved drama, especially drama
> of a nature shocking to other people. She heard a woman confess
> her sins, loudly proclaiming such petty errors as bilking London
> Transport, fraudulent practice with regard to her housekeeping
> money, and visits to a theatre. How much better than that she
> could do! She was forty, and even she could see that, with her
> faded fair hair and fine pale skin, she hadn't worn well. What
> next? A grim obscure domesticity in Harlesden . . . or the
> glorious publicity the Epiphany People could give her. Besides
> it [their beliefs] might all be true. Very soon she was to be-
> lieve entirely in its truth. (p. 70)

For the first time in her life, perhaps, Joan can readily
feel superior to almost everyone else, and feel superior she
does, denouncing the "sins" of others, demanding that they
think and behave as she does. Most of them, of course, do
not, and that reaction, too, feeds Joan's sense of drama and
self-importance:

> This birdlike, bright-haired, bright-spirited little body was
> . . . devoured with curiosity about her fellow men. . . . She
> also suffered from a particular form of paranoia. She projected
> her feelings onto the Lord. A devout woman must not be unchar-
> itable, so she seldom indulged her dislike of people by straight
> malicious gossip. It was not she who found them and hated them,
> but God; not she but God on whom they had inflicted imaginary
> injuries. "Vengeance is mine, saith the Lord: I will repay."
> Joan Smith was merely his humble and energetic instrument. (p. 62)

As Giles' search for religion draws him closer to humanity, Joan's sets her ever more apart from, ever more "above," her fellows. Despite her constant, harrowing habit of "quoting" scripture, Joan doesn't really study or understand the Bible; instead, she speaks in elevated biblical language, bending the ideas she occasionally finds there to suit her own purposes-- "The Son of Man cometh like a thief in the night, but the foolish virgin has let her lamp go out" (p. 92).

Giles, on the other hand, does study the religions he considers: when he is intent on India and a begging bowl, he reads the *Bhagavad Gita* and the *Upanishads*; when he becomes interested in Catholicism, he switches, equally seriously, to Newman. Now Giles is, as has been demonstrated, neither a hero nor a fanatic, and, true to Rendell's realism and to the boy's character, the first impulses of his search are humorous and arise from his daydreams.

> Now he was on his way to Sudbury to buy a packet of orange dye. He was going to dye all his jeans and T-shirts orange in pursuance of his religion, which was, roughly, Buddhism. When he had saved up enough money he meant to go to India on a bus. . . . That is, if he didn't become a Catholic instead. He had just finished reading *Brideshead Revisited* and had begun to wonder whether being a Catholic at Oxford and burning incense on one's staircase might not be better than India. But he'd dye the jeans and T-shirts just in case. (p. 17)

Waugh and opportunity have their effect, and Giles switches to dreams of his romantic concept of life as a Catholic:

> Disillusionment over India had killed Oriental religion for Giles. It would never, anyway, have fitted with his plans for himself and Melinda. He saw them sharing their flat, devout Catholics both, but going through agonies to maintain their chaste and continent condition. Perhaps he would become a priest, and if Melinda were to enter a convent they might--say twice a year--have special dispensation to meet and, soberly garbed, have tea together in some humble cafe, not daring to touch hands. Or like Lancelot and Guinevere, but without the preceding pleasures, encounter each other across a cathedral nave, gaze long and long, then part without a word. Before becoming a priest, he must become a Catholic, and he was looking around Stantwich for someone to give him instruction. (pp. 93-94)

Indeed, without discussing it with anyone, Giles does undertake instruction, and, interestingly, his daydreams diminish after he does so. He seems to be taking this venture into faith seriously, and as Rendell has shwon us, it may well influence his growing toterance for and understanding of his stepfather. It may also lessen, marginally, the despair--if not the awfulness--of his death: "For the last time Giles saw the Elevation of the Mass. Although he was not yet received into the Church, kind Father Madigan had heard his confession and shriven him, and Giles was perhaps in a state of grace" (p. 144).

Always an ironist, Rendell does not present Giles' faith as an answer or a panacea; however, she shows readers that it can be contrasted with Joan Smith's hectic, devastating commitment. A recent convert, Giles is still feeling his way

into true belief, but it has already helped him to grow. A
late convert, Joan Smith is confirmed in her beliefs, but they
have not really changed her. Rather, they have merely re-
channeled her selfishness, exacerbated her insanity: "She had
reached the edge of a pit in which was nothing short of raving
madness, and she teetered there on the brink until ... whipped-
up fanaticism toppled her over" (p. 96), and shortly after one
of her dramatic displays at an Epiphany People meeting, she
precipitates the murders. The contrast between Joan, a killer,
and Giles, her victim, is complete.

Thus, in her portrait of Giles Mont, Rendell has firmly
joined characterization and plot. Generating a subplot, con-
tributing to the main plot as victim and complication, Giles
also serves as contrast to the venemous Joan. Further, through
her exploration of his character, the author has dramatized
much of the development of an important theme: the impact of
religion. The presence of Giles, that gentle ghost, helps
keep a highly intellectual book well within the realm of good
story telling, and that is no small achievement.

A Judgement in Stone is a strong novel, representing a
major category in Rendell's canon; it is a serious novel,
raising serious questions, stimulating and touching. It explores one rather exaggerated but useful form of the isolation
inherent in the human condition and depicts the youthful outsider as eventual joiner and sharer. It reveals the author's
skill, for the novel is enormously enhanced by Ruth Rendell's
merging of characterization and narrative thrust.

RUNNING HOT AND COLD WITH RON FAUST

BY GEORGE KELLEY

Ron Faust writs about survival.

His books usually include a murder or six, but at the heart of things is the battle to survive not only the threat of the burderer, but also the hostile environment that's as deadly as any murderer.

Faust's first novel, *Tombs of Blue Ice* (Bobbs-Merrill, 1974), is set in the French Alps. Robert Holmes, a free-lance writer and mountain climber, finds his climbing party destroyed as a bolt of lightning blasts them while they huddle against a bitter storm, clinging to the side of a mountain. One of the climbers dies instantly; Holmes is only shaken up, but the third member, Dieter Streicher, has a broken leg. Holmes leaves Streicher to get help. When help arrives on the peak, Streicher is gone.

Holmes gets involved in the search for Streicher, but he soon learns Streicher was the son of a hated German Occupation leader. The people of the little French valley have long memories. The book moves briskly to the final confrontation between Holmes and the murderer above and below the Alpine snows.

In Faust's next book, *The Wolfe in the Clouds* (Bobbs-Merrill, 1977; Popular Library, 1980), Jack Marty, skier for the U.S. Forest Service, battles against a homicidal maniac and the killer avalanches of the Colorado mountains.

Jack and fellow-skier Frank Treblene head into the Colorado mountains to look for three college students missing since a violent snowstorm hit. Jack and Frank are warned against the rescue mission by the police, who are searching for Ralph Brace, a former Forest Service skier who's just murdered fourteen people by shooting them while they rode the ski-lift chairs to the top of the slopes, just like ducks in a shooting gallery. Ralph Brace still lurks in the mountains with his telescopic rifle.

Jack and Frank still attempt the rescue and find the college students holed up in an isolated cabin high in the mountains. And Ralph Brace finds them all.

The Wolfe in the Clouds presents a chilling story of a deadly psychopath and the struggle against the odds to survive the killer and the deadly mountains. This is one of Faust's best books.

Faust shifts gears in *The Burning Sky* (Playboy, 1978). Gone are the paragraphs of expert commentary on mountain climbing techniques and methods of avalanche control. Ben Pearce is a New Mexico rancher who's future is threatened by law suits, back taxes, and an encroaching civilization bent on destroying the wildness of the land and the wildness of Ben Pearce.

Ben tries to make a last-ditch attempt to save his land: he agrees to lead a Texas millionaire, his insane wife, and their troubled son on a hunt for illegal game: a leopard, a jaguar, and a mountain lion.

Under a burning sky, Pearce and the Stuart family hunt the dangerous animals and play their deadly games that inevitably end in death. This is a powerful book peopled by carefully

11

drawn characters.

The Long Count (Fawcett, 1979) is Faust's best book to date. Jim Racine is an over-the-hill U.S. boxer who's come out of retirement for one more series of fights in South America and Latin America. But in an old bullring, in the sweaty heat and screams of the crowd, Racine kills a young fighter when the referee refuses to stop the match. Racine's in trouble.

The U.S. ambassador pulls Racine's passport. After weeks of trying, Racine finally sees the ambassador after a late-night party. The ambassador invites Racine to ride back to the embassy with his party of workers and staff. On the ride back, the limousine is hijacked by terrorists. Some of the party are killed right off, but Racine, the ambassador, and a few others are spared.

Complications set in: the negotiations drag on, the terrorists are divided, and Racine plots his surviving in the steaming jungles. *The Long Count* features some of Faust's best writing and powerful story-telling.

Faust's latest book, *Death Fires* (Fawcett, 1980), takes place in the white heat of Baja. In a small Mexican coastal village, a team of movie production technicians and actors are taking part in a murderous drama directed by a madman.

Death Fires is told in the third person by Julian Campbell, the cinematographer. (All of Faust's previous novels are first-person narrations.) Julian is prone to have blackouts, fugues, during which he can't remember what he has done. The actress is Sharon Saunders, a troubled young woman. The director is insane: for Alfredo DiMotta, a death can't be faked-- it must be real. As this strange company works on the film, a man dies, and violence seeths below the surface.

Events become even more deadly when DiMotta strands Julian and Sharon in the ocean on a small boat to film them dying. Faust's theme of individual survival is here, with a mix of kinky sex and madness. Unfortunately, the mix doesn't quite jell. *Death Fires* has some intense moments, but the conception isn't as complete as *The Burning Sky* and *The Long Count*.

Ron Faust is an ambitious writer with talent and interesting stories to tell, a combination that makes him worth reading.

SPEAKING WITH MYSELF

BY BILLY BARTON

[Mr. Barton is an internationally famous circus performer, a trap-
eze artist turned mystery novelist. His first book, *Past Murder
Imperfect,* published by his own company Bilbar Books, is currently
on the market. He is unmarried and lives alone.]

Q: I wish you'd tell me why we're having this interview in
the first place. Seems rather silly to me.

A: Most things I do seem silly to you. We're having this
interview because I am tired of being misquoted. I want to
set the record straight. Unfortunately, most interviews are
conducted where I am performing my aerial act. I am expected
to be *on,* like a freak attraction with two heads. For once I
want to sound like *me.*

Q: (Dubiously) Well . . . if you wish to make an ass out
of yourself, I guess there's nothing I can do to stop you.
I've never had much influence with you before.

A: Look, friend, spare me the usual lecturing--just get
down to it. And refrain from asking questions about the circus. I'm sick of talking about circus.

Q: Here goes then . . . . Do you consider yourself a
mystery fan?

A: Yes, but mostly of detection novels, puzzle plots.
Funny thing, though, I never considered myself a mystery addict
prior to writing mysteries. I guess, like Christie, I feel
that once you start a life of crime you can't stop.

Q: Is that the only reason?

A: No. I like a story with a beginning, a middle, and an
end. A detection novel can't be abstract. And what some
critics call old-fashioned, I call fundamentally good story-
telling. In each of the arts exist principles that remain
constant; to change them courts disaster. The ingredients of
a circus, for example, consist of elephants, clowns, aerial-
ists. Remove the basics, and its no longer a circus. Same
thing with mystery fiction . . . .

Q: I thought we weren't going to bring up "circus."

A: Sorry.

Q: Don't do it again.

A: I'll try not to.

Q: Why did you begin writing detection novels?

A: I started because Agatha Christie died and no other
writer furnished me the same enjoyment. I like a plot with
lots of complication, a puzzle, a surprize, and a final twist.
At this, Christie was spectacularly consistent. Even when she
was bad she never failed?

Q: Are *you* consistent?

A: God knows I try to be. If a book doesn't measure up,
it's restructured or discarded. Months and months of *hard*
labor go into plotting. I diagram and cross check. It's
essential to know *precisely* where I'm headed.

Q: What are your working habits?

A: (Laughingly) As if *you* didn't know. You nag me enough!

Q: Yes, yes, *I* know, but readers don't, so tell *them.*

A: The last chapters are written first, but loosely, so
new points can be tied in. No matter how thoroughly worked up

the plot, ideas develop which must be incorporated. The first
chapter is written next, many times, until polished. For me,
the first chapter is the most difficult, the most important.
More important is the opening paragraph. After that, the entire book is written straight at the typewriter, with minimal
rereading and minimal re-working. Then it is permitted to
jell for at least two weeks--longer, if possible. Finally,
it is reread, analyzed, checked for loose ends, proofed once
for content, again for spelling and punctuation, and again for
ambiguities, redundancies, and inconsistencies; in my first
book, for example, I have a character rising from a chair whom
I have quite forgotten to seat! When a work is in progress,
nothing other than a dire emergency is allowed to interrupt.
The phone is turned off, no performing engagements are booked,
and a strict schedule is adhered to. I don't believe in writer's block. Blockage is merely a warning to take a hard look
at what has been written; something is wrong. Writers waiting
for inspiration are not professionals, they're procrastinators.
A pro works even when he is not in the mood, when he is not
functioning at his best. I have performed my aerial act with
a broken foot, the flue, and torn muscles. It's all a matter
of discipline and dedication.

Q: Does the lack of a formal education bother you?

A: No, but I think it bothers you. I just have to work
harder to be a careful writer.

Q: Was it your grandmother who instilled in you a love of
all things British? The British mystery in particular?

A: I'm sure she had much to do with my affinity for the
English, and they are experts at the puzzle plot.

Q: Why is it that Americans are not so accomplished in
that type story?

A: Americans think unlike the British. Our life styles
are different. Our country is a melting pot of varied cul-
tures, a true mixed bag. But Americans excel in other areas.
Did we not invent the hard-boiled school? Its a fair exchange.

Q: Yet you, an American, write like an Englishman.

A: My grandmother, who reared me, was a dyed-in-the-wool
Englishwoman if ever one existed! She also was my tutor. She
had been a Shakespearean actress before immigrating to America;
she was brilliantly educated. In my first book, the character
Adalaide Arthur is modeled on my grandmother and not, as
everyone assumes, on Agatha Christie. Grandmother was not
only English to the core but also was married to a transplanted
Scotsman, so my genes are not all that scrambled.

Q: I happen to know that your father had a dalliance with
a French woman. You were the result.

A: What a sneaky way to call me a bastard! But I never
knew her. I know only that she came from Ontario--a very English province--and I suspect that she, too, may have had English blood.

Q: And I suspect you simply want to be thought of as an
Englishman.

A: What I really want to be thought of as is an American
handling the buzzle plot as well as the British.

Q: Does being compared to Christie flatter you? Are you
concerned that Christie fans might be offended? And how did
that comparison evolve?

A: Naturally I am flattered. No, I'm sure Christie fans
won't be offended. I've had letters from many, even from those

in England, all expressing pleasure with the book. When the
book was making its rounds, being judged by professionals,
that's all we heard: "It reads like a Christie." We heard it
so often and for so long, especially when it was in galleys,
that a decision was made to use the Christie thing on the
jacket and in the advance advertising. Truth is, my book is
a tribute to Christie.
Q: You self-published. Was it difficult?
A: Publishing wasn't difficult; the difficulties cropped
up *after* publication and *after* we had exhausted marketing
ideas for the first edition. Knowledge and experience came
later, with the second printing, through hindsight and from
new friends in the book business.
Q: Did you have an agent? Are agents necessary?
A: Yes, I had an agent. And while agents are not necessary, they can be exceedingly helpful. My agent was not. She
felt that I was out of my element, that what I was writing was
"unrealistic," which amused me when I learned she peddled man-
uscripts to a famed house specializing in paperback romances.
How unrealistic can you get? Besides, who needs realism? Our
sensibilities are revolted by enough in our daily newspapers
and on the evening news.
Q: Do you resent the term "tea cozies"?
A: I think it's a put down. My book was called a cozy by
one reviewer and it infuriated me. It isn't. Not all of
Christie's books are, either. But people love to label things.
I just hope they remember that Christie is the all-time best-
selling mystery writer. Somebody out there enjoys playing
cozy and sipping tea!
Q: What won't you put in your books?
A: Sex, filthy language, a predominant love theme, violence for the sake of violence. And kids. I can't write about
children, can't relate to them. My first book has a scene with
a child. It was glossed over--quickly?
Q: What, other than twists and surprises, are prerequisites?
A: Playing scrupulously fair, laying out all the clues,
dealing with characters in an economical manner, not allowing
background to obtrude, concentrating on plot.
Q: Do you write to please yourself?
A: First, last, and always. When one attempts to please
everyone, he pleases no one.
Q: Are you happy with your first book?
A: (Sighing) Is anyone ever happy with *any* book? PMI was
a difficult book to do. It has a double plot; it's actually
two novels in one. I never would attempt such an ambitious
undertaking again. I am, however, satisfied with the way it
is structured, and there isn't a thing about it I would change
or let be changed. I have corrected some minor details my
editor missed for the paperback reprint, but most of my dis-
satisfaction stemmed from incompetent typesetters. We are
putting my new book into type ourselves, so that problem has
been resolved.
Q: How do you feel about critics and book reviewers?
A: Most are intelligent people doing an important service.
But a review, good or bad, is only one opinion and must be
taken at face value. If a review is good so much the better,
but any review helps spread the word, and even a knock is a
boost.
Q: Other than Christie, who is your favorite mystery author?

A: I don't have one. I try to read a little of every writer I can. It's important to know who's who and what's what. Of current writers I enjoy Catherine Aird. I liked P.D. James until I read *Innocent Blood,* which is well written but boring. She's gone snobbish on us, I think. Ngaio Marsh's *Grave Mistake* is one of her finest efforts. There are writers I simply cannot read at all. But I won't mention them.

Q: What are your favorite Christies?

A: Probably the ones nobody else thinks of as her best, those receiving the least recognition. *Ackroyd* is a trick, albeit a great one, but I do not agree that it is her master-piece. *Nile* is strewn with plot holes, and *Murder on the Links* is a manual for what *not* to do in a detection novel. It is easily the worst thing she ever wrote. Unbelievable and unforgivable, the errors in that book! But I adore *Styles,* which hangs together well because she was forced to rewrite the last third and then forced to make additional alterations. Christie *needed* an editor, if only to see that she tied up all those loose ends. She was careless in many areas. What got her off the hook was her story-telling genius.

Q: You talk mostly about women. Don't you know any men?

A: In equal numbers, I'd say. But I happen to like women, and my entire life has come under positive feminine influence. First, my grandmother; later, Mae West; and, indirectly, Christie.

Q: What about male mystery authors?

A: Other than Doyle, in the puzzle field they rate second best. Many won't agree, but I don't expect them to. I'm stating a belief to which I'm entitled, so I hope I don't get letters taking me to task.

Q: Oh, come now! There must be *one* male mystery writer you admire.

A: All right! Oscar Wilde. In many ways *Dorian Gray* is a perfect mystery novel.

Q: What are your future writing plans?

A: The new book is ready, the third is plotted, the two to follow are in outline. I work on two books simultaneously. Exhausted by one, I turn to the other to derive a peculiar sort of rejuvenation.

Q: Are all those books titled?

A: Yes.

Q: Do you ever change them?

A: No, and nobody else had better try.

Q: What do you feel is the secret of good writing?

A: Cutting hell out of everything and removing the parts one likes best.

Q: How do you take to constructive criticism?

A: I'm learning to appreciate it, but I don't have to like it, do I? I'm guided by instinct. My circus background has taught me valuable timing, pacing, showmanship, and other techniques which I apply to my writing craft. If the perform-ance is too long, if the acts are set in the wrong place, the spectator gets restless, leaves. Also, I keep my books to a *readable length.*

Q: Briefly describe your new book.

A: It's a comedy-mystery.

Q: Not always a workable hybrid.

A: No, but it can be accomplished, and I like a challenge. The comedy, however, arises from situation. It isn't just stuck in.

Q: Is Jason Conover in it? Is he your series detective?

A: Yes, and no; he's in it, but he is not a series detective. I don't have one. Tiresome, you realize, to be
forced to use the same character again and again. I couldn't
retain him anyway, because I made the same mistake as Christie: Jason started out too old. For me to keep using Jason,
he would have to discover immortality, and that *is* straining
credulity. I prefer continuing characters, ordinary people
with whom readers may identify. Seven characters from my
first book are in my second.

Q: How long will you go on with your performing career?

A: Another year. Combining the two professions is a gim-
mick that grabs media attention. And it is trye that I am
the first circus performer to become a novelist, although
everyone expected me to write about the circus.

Q: Will you?

A: Later, perhaps . . . when I can look back objectively.

Q: What about an autobiography?

A: You do it, you're always butting in anyway.

Q: You ramble a lot, did you know that?

A: That's your fault. You're asking the questions. Besides, I didn't talk us into this--*you* did.

It's About Crime

By Marvin Lachman

There are millions of people who read mysteries but probably fewer than a thousand who get as much (or more) pleasure reading about them. You're one of the latter or you wouldn't be reading TMF. Therefore, you are aware of all the magazines and books about your favorite kind of literature which have been published since 1967. Now comes Jon L. Breen with a book about books about mysteries. It's called *What About Murder?* and it has just been published at $10.00 by Scarecrow Press (52 Liberty St., P.O. Box 656, Metuchen, NJ 08840).

Don't think that this is some attempt to cash in on a trend. This is an indispensable guide to 239 books, including encyclopedias, histories, critiques, writing manuals, and biographies. Breen appears to have read thoroughly every book he discusses. As a result, he has produced a work that is accurate and contains well-thought-out opinions. Breen is devastating regarding the books he considers poor, and that is a virtue because the potential buyer is spared possible expense. He is also very current, including books published during the latter part of 1980. Best of all, *What About Murder?* is fun to read. Breen imparts information and opinion without ever being dry.

Incidentally, has anyone noticed that Jon Breen has quietly become just about the soundest mystery reviewer around?

Recently, I went on vacation with only one mystery to read, and I had tough going until I could find a store at which I could get a "fix." The book was Michael Innes's *From London Far* (1946; U.S. title, *The Unsuspected Chasm*), and it started promisingly. A British language scholar stumbles into the headquarters of the International Society for the Diffusion of Cultural Objects, an organization stealing paintings and statues in war-ravaged Europe. Very shortly, a grand chase ensues, and the scholar is falling off a scaffold, holding on to the tongue (!) of a large, ineffective bloodhound.

This book is one of the oddest amalgams I've read, since it combines dozens of literary allusions with occasional breakneck slapstick. Ultimately, it doesn't work at all. Innes's plotting is almost non-existent. For every bit of inspired craziness--e.g., the professor who is sure he is being followed by pantechnicons (vans to us Yanks)--there are pages of aimless talk, much of it in incomprehensible Scottish dialect. There is also outrageous coincidence and the kind of dumb hero who keeps everything a secret from the police.

18

Literary opposites attract, so I turned to William Campbell Gault, about as far from Michael Innes as one can get. Gault's *Don't Cry for Me* won him an Edgar for Best First Novel of 1952, and it launched ten years of some of the best hard-boiled writing this side of Chandler. Discouraged at no longer being able to sell in the mid-1960's, Gault restrict his output to juvenile books. However, I understand he recently sold a mystery novel, to which we can all look forward.

Gault's here, Pete Worden, is a former USC football star (anticipating his creator's series character, Brock Callahan) who must turn amateur detective. He is a well-rounded character who grows during the course of the book. The best thing in *Don't Cry for Me* is the way it evokes Los Angeles at a specific time, December 1950. Gault uses the Korean War, the NFL playoffs, and Christmas in a warm climate to give us a word picture that will tell readers in 2050 what it was like. However, the important thing is that Gault's socio-history is just a bonus to a good mystery.

Unconsciously, the book says something else about its times. The book uses the words "bull deletion" and "horse deletion" during conversations between two genuinely tough people. I'm no advocate of random cursing, but I wonder if anyone would really have been that offended, even in 1952, if someone published the words "bull shit" and "horse shit."

I suspect that Mike Seidman's lamentations regarding the future of the mystery raised more controversy than any other panel comments at Bouchercon 1980. Not to worry. If some of the recent reprints are any indication, we'll have more good books to read than we can get to in our lives.

Dover, even without Ev Bleiler, continues to show imagination in their selections and outstanding taste in the appearance and durability of their paper covers. Their books are a joy to anyone who loves books. They've specialized in short stories and have just come out with the first U.S. paperback reprint of the only volume of Philip Trent stories, *Trent Intervenes* (1938), by E.C. Bentley, for $4.00. Not too long ago, they did a splendid collection of Roy Vickers shorts, *Department of Dead Ends* (1978), for $3.50, which is still in print. Outstanding in this group of well-plotted procedurals are "A Toy for Jiffy" and "Little Things Like That," the latter being a wonderful story about the results of an anxiety complex.

Dover has not neglected the novel. Just arrived, too late to be read for this column, are Francis Beeding's classic *Death Walks in Eastrepps* (1931), at $4.00, and Cyril Hare's first mystery, *A Tenant in Death* (1937), at $3.50.

Dell, using the names of famous mystery book stores, has launched two interesting series: MURDER INK and SCENE OF THE CRIME. Most of the titles are reprints of recent British books, but a few show some real imagination, e.g., Jane Langton's *The Transcendental Murder* (1964; a.k.a. *The Minuteman Murder*), $2.25, set in Concord, Massachusetts. Langton, like Gault better known for her children's books, accomplishes the almost impossible feat of weaving philosophy and American history so carefully into the plot of a fine story that not a single seam shows. Just imagine a modern day murder in which Emily Dickinson, Ralph Waldo Emerson, Henry Thoreau, and Louisa May Alcott are characters.

For quantity and quality it's hard to beat the Harper

Perennial Library series. The following is merely a sample of
what is already in the book stores, with more to come:

1. Julian Symons, *The 31st of February*, 1950, $1.95. As
off-beat as its title; an expressionist painting of a novel.
Don't miss it.

2. E.C. Bentley, *Trent's Last Case*, 1913, $1.95, and, with
H. Warner Allen, *Trent's Own Case*, 1936, $2.25. These are the
other two books in the Trent series. *Trent's Last Case* was
probably THE major influence on the Golden Age of the detective story.

3. Nicholas Blake, *The Beast Must Die*, 1938, $1.95. Read
the first few pages and see if you can avoid identifying with
the protagonist. Also, *Smiler with the Knife*, 1939, $1.95.
Probably comes as close to duplicating the pace and subject
matter of early Hitchcock movies as one can do within the
pages of a book.

4. Andrew Garve, *The Cuckoo-Line Affair*, 1953, *The Riddle
of Samson*, 1954, *A Hero for Leanda*, 1959, and *The Ashes of Loda*,
1965. An author who almost always surprises and uses natural
settings better than almost anyone else. *Loda* contains a
great chase scene in Russia. *Cuckoo-Line* is typical of Garve
in that the amateur detective has a believable reason for investigating, not merely an inclination to meddle.

It's no secret that by the mid-1970's the Perry Mason
books of Erle Stanley Gardner were no longer selling. Pocket
Books, Inc., tried combining two novels under one set of covers but apparently without real success. Now, a new publisher,
Ballantine, is trying to rescue the series from what Dannay
used to call "biblivion."

I've a soft spot in my head--er, I mean heart--for Perry
Mason and friends. I've read them all and enjoyed the action
and the courtroom shenanigans. The series was at its best
from 1933 to 1945, with occasional later bright spots. Ballantine has launched its reprints with the cases of the *Lazy
Lover* (1947), *Fiery Fingers* (1951), *Daring Divorcee* (1964),
and *Beautiful Beggar* (1965), at $1.95 apiece. While all are
readable, they are far from being the best selection of Mason
mysteries. Also, it just goes against my sense of the natural
order of things to begin with numbers thirty, thirty-seven,
seventy-two, and seventy-six in the series. Let's reprint
that foundation of my misbegotten education, *The Case of the
Velvet Claws* (1933).

Mystery * File
Short Reviews
By Steve Lewis

Catherine Aird. *Passing Strange*. Doubleday/Crime Club, 1981, 174 pp., $9.95.

In the same category as Mary Fitt of a generation earlier, Catherine Aird is another writer whose works others have been praising highly to me. If this latest book of hers is typical, however, once again I am dense, and I fail to see what the shouting's all about.

The detective in most of her books is Inspector Sloan, of the Criminal Investigation Department of the Berebury Division of the Calleshire Force. Here he investigates the death of the village nurse, by strangulation, at the annual Almstone Flower and Horticultural Show, a gala event in this section of Britain. At stake is the proper identification of a would-be heiress to a large estate, but what it is that provides Sloan with the key to the killer is a tray laden with food and the matter of the labels that were switched on the show's prize-winning tomatoes.

In terms of loving portrayals of rural English eccentric-ities, I was reminded at first of Edmund Crispin's tales of the redoubtable and resourceful Gervase Fen, but Aird's brand of wackiness soon turned significantly more cynical, and its charms were eventually lost in the clutter of tediously inter-changeable village people.

While the story is competently told, it simply lacks the appearance of striving for any particular heights. There are a few sparks of wit that are struck, but they never seem to catch fire. The whole affair is already fading badly from memory, and by the time another month rolls around, I suspect it will have been all but forgotten. (C plus)

Mary Ann Taylor. *Red Is for Shrouds*. Raven House, 1980, 186 pp., $1.75.

This second Raven House mystery is, if nothing else, a good sight better than the first one, *Crimes Past*, by Mary Challis, reviewed a couple of issues ago. (It was Jeff Meyer-son, by the way, who was the first to suggest to me that "Mary Challis" is actually Sara Woods. The evidence is strongly convincing.)

I haven't heard of Mary Ann Taylor before now either--much of the Raven House line seems to consist of unknowns and/or

writers hiding with obvious embarrassment under phoney by-
lines--but she has a follow-up to this one out already. It
also takes place in the small town of Bolton, exact location
unknown, but apparently somewhere in the western plains: *Return to Murder*, Raven House #23.

Police Chief Emil Martin puts his career on the line in
this one. A series of murders has nearly wiped out the town's
population of red-haired women, and murder is a crime that
Martin has hardly had much experience with. After a while
the townspeople start getting antsy, and in a very real sense
it is he who finds himself on trial.

By category you'd have to call this a police procedural,
but it's a down-home folksy sort of one that big-city inhab-
itants aren't going to enjoy and appreciate half as much as
those with small-town roots. By nature, it's also a puzzle
story, and as such the surprise comes a bit at the expense of
the characters as they've been constructed up to then--but
only a bit.

Good, wholesome mystery entertainment. (C plus)

William X. Kienzle. *Mind over Murder*. Andrews & McMeel,
1981, 296 pp., $9.95.

As a former priest himself, William Kienzle knows a lot
about the Roman Catholic Church, its weaker points and human
failings as well as its many successes. The murder of a
priest for reasons concerning his occupation, no matter how
self-serving his actions and motives, is still a matter of
staggering magnitude in concept alone--not to mention its
actual fulfillment.

This is the handicap Kienzle places upon himself as a
writer, from very nearly page one on. Without the right touch,
without an eye for the humor in a delicate situation, without
being convincingly sure of himself, another writer might have
led this premise straight into disaster.

The victim-to-be is obvious from the start. Monsignor
Tommy Thompson is the director of the Tribunal, the archdio-
cesan matrimonial court for the city of Detroit and environs.
As such, it is he who must make the decisions as to whether or
not annulments should be granted to marriages which have
failed. Tommy Thompson, however, operates as much by whim and
a grasping desire for power as he does by canonical law, and a
lot of innocent people can, and do, get their lives messed up
rather badly by his judgments.

At least five of them sit down and, separately, plot his
murder. After his disappearance, under extremely suspicious
circumstances, each of their problems is found to have been
intimately written up in Thompson's diary. With both of Detroit's leading newspapers hot on the story, "The Case of the
Missing Monsignor" becomes a whodunit for the whole state of
Michigan to follow.

Kienzle has let his imagination go to work in this latest
Father Koesler thriller. In spite of what seems at times to
border on heresy, he obviously loves the people that belong to
and are a part of his religion. He is equally in agreement
with its basic philosophies, if not always with the ways they
are carried out.

He also tells a gripping and fairly played detective story.

BOOKS FOR SALE

Do not send money with order. Instead, enclose a self-addressed postcard or stamped envelope which I can use to advise you of which books were still available and how much you owe. Please remit promptly; I won't wait for your check to ship the books, but I'd appreciate your sending it to me at your very earliest convenience. Postage is $1.00 for the first hardbound book ($1.00 for the first two paperbacks), and $.50 for each additional hardback ($.25 for each two additional paperbacks) up to a maximum postage charge of $3.00. Send your orders to Guy M. Townsend, 29 S. Church St., West Chester, PA 19380.

HARDBOUND, DUST-JACKETED REVIEW COPIES, FINE TO MINT CONDITION, $2.50 EACH:
Leslie Andress, CAPER, Putnam's, 1980.
Carolyn Banks, THE DARKROOM, Viking, 1980.
John Burmeister, THE HARD MEN, St. Martin's, 1978.
Richard Butler, LIFT-OFF AT SATAN, St. Martin's, 1979.
William Camp, THE JACOBS PARK KILLINGS, Vanguard, 1978.
Rodney Campbell, THE LUCIANO PROJECT, McGraw-Hill, 1977 (non-fiction).
Robin Cook, COMA, Little, Brown, 1977.
Robin Cook, SPHINX, Putnam's, 1979.
Oliver Crawford, THE EXECUTION, St. Martin's, 1978.
Celia Dale, THE DECEPTION, Harper, 1979.
Thomas L. Dunne, THE SCOURGE, Coward, McCann, & Geoghegan, 1978.
Digby Durrant, WITH MY LITTLE EYE, St. Martin's, 1978.
Paul Durst, THE FLORENTINE TABLE, Scribner's, 1980.
Erich Erdstein, with Barbara Bean, INSIDE THE FOURTH REICH, St. Martins, 1978 (non-fiction).
Kenneth L. Evans, A FEAST FOR SPIDERS, Crowell, 1979.
Hugh Fleetwood, THE REDEEMER, Atheneum, 1980.
Edward Franklin, MAN ON THE WIRE, Crown, 1978.
Tony Foster, ZIG ZAG TO ARMAGEDDON, Ermine, 1978.
Sandor Fankel & Webster Mews, THE ALEPH SOLUTION, Stein & Day, 1978.
Laurence Halley, SIMULTANEOUS EQUATIONS, St. Martin's, 1978.
R.E. Harrington, QUINTAIN, Putnam's, 1977.
Joanne Hoppe, THE LESSON IS MURDER, Harcourt, Brace, Jovanovich, 1977.
Jim Hougan, SPOOKS: THE HAUNTING OF AMERICA—THE PRIVATE USE OF SECRET AGENTS, Morrow, 1978 (non-fiction).
Jon A. Jackson, THE DIEHARD, Random House, 1977.
Christopher Keane, THE CROSSING, Arbor House, 1978.
Richard W. Larsen, BUNDY: THE DELIBERATE STRANGER, Prentice Hall, 1980 (non-fiction).
Roy Lewis, AN UNCERTAIN SOUND, St. Martin's, 1980.
David Lippincott, SAVAGE RANSOM, Rawson, 1978.
James Broom Lynne, JET RACE, Putnam's, 1978.
Ulf Miehe, PUMA, St. Martin's, 1978.
Walter Nelson, THE SIEGE OF BUCKINGHAM PALACE, Little, Brown, 1979.
Thomas Page, SIGMET ACTIVE, Times Books, 1978.
Larry Pryor, THE VIPER, Harper & Row, 1978.
Ritchie Perry, GRAND SLAM, Pantheon, 1980.
Denis Pitts, ROGUE HERCULES, Atheneum, 1978.
Marion Rippon, LUCIEN'S TOMBS, Doubleday/Crime Club, 1979.
Mara Rostov, NIGHT HUNT, Putnam's, 1979.
John Rowe, THE ASWAN SOLUTION, Doubleday, 1979.
Rosemarie Santini, ABRACADABRA, Playboy Press, 1977.
Tony Scaduto, A TERRIBLE TIME TO DIE, Putnam's 1978.
Jack S.Scott, THE SHALLOW GRAVE, Harper & Row, 1978.
Michael Sinclair, THE MASTERPLAYERS, Norton, 1978.
Nigel Slater, FALCON, Atheneum, 1979.

Irwin Philip Sobel, DR. MONTE CRISTO, Doubleday, 1978.
Anthony Stuart, THAT MAN GULL, Arbor House, 1977.
Anthony Stuart, VICIOUS CIRCLES, Arbor House, 1979.
Sydney Smith, THE SURVIROR, St. Martin's, 1979.
Walter Stovall, PRESIDENTIAL EMERGENCY, Dutton, 1978.
Raymond Thompson & Treve Daly, THE NUMBER TO CALL IS..., St. Martin's, 1979.
John Wainwright, THE VENUS FLY-TRAP, St. Martin's, 1980.

PAPERBACKS--UNREAD REVIEW COPIES IN FINE TO MINT CONDITION, $1.00 EACH:
Albert Barker, GIFT FROM BERLIN, Charter, 1980.
Robert Barnard, DEATH OF A MYSTERY WRITER, Dell Scene of the Crime, 1980.
Robert Barnard, DEATH ON THE HIGH C'S, Dell Scene of the Crime, 1981.
Anthony Berkeley, TRIAL AND ERROR, Dell Scene of the Crime, 1981.
John Dickson Carr, HE WHO WHISPERS, Charter [1980].
Leslie Charteris, THE SAINT IN ACTION, Charter, 1980.
Leslie Charteris, THE SAINT INTERVENES, Charter, 1981.
Agatha Christie, MR. PARKER PYNE, DETECTIVE, Dell, 1981.
V.C. Clinton-Baddeley, ONLY A MATTER OF TIME, Dell Murder Ink, 1981.
Kent Cooper, BELOW HOUSTON STREET, Manor, 1978.
John Creasey, SALUTE THE TOFF, Charter, 1980.
Elizabeth Daly, DEATH AND LETTERS, Dell Murder Ink, 1981.
Anthony Esler, HELLBANE, Fawcett Crest, c. 1978.
Séan Flannery, EAGLES FLY, Charter, 1980.
Dick Francis, ODDS AGAINST, Pocket, c. 1980.
Dick Francis, SLAYRIDE, Pocket, c. 1979.
Erle Stanley Gardner, TCOT BEAUTIFUL BEGGAR, Ballantine, 1981.
Erle Stanley Gardner, TCOT DARING DIVORCEE, Ballantine, 1981.
Erle Stanley Gardner, TCOT FIERY FINGERS, Ballantine, 1981.
Erle Stanley Gardner, TCOT LAZY LOVER, Ballantine, 1981.
Bartholomew Gill, MCGARR AND THE SIENESE CONSPIRACY, Dell Murder Ink, 1980.
Bartholomew Gill, MCGARR AND THE DUBLIN HORSE SHOW, Dell Murder Ink, 1981.
Joe Gores, DEAD SKIP, Ballantine, 1981.
Henry Henn, ATHERWOOD TERMINAL, Manor, 1978.
James Hilton, WAS IT MURDER? Perennial, 1980.
Robert Holles, SPAWN, Berkeley, 1980.
Hammond Innes, AIR BRIDGE, Ballantine, 1979.
Hammond Innes, THE DOOMED OASIS, Ballantine, 1978.
Hammond Innes, LEVKAS MAN, Ballantine, 1979.
Hammond Innes, NORTH STAR, Ballantine, 1979.
Hammond Innes, THE STRODE VENTURER, Ballantine, 1979.
Dave Klein, BLIND SIDE, Charter, 1980.
Stephen Kral, POWER GAME, Playboy, 1979.
Edwin D. Krell & Maj. J.J. Vasel, KILLER COPS, Manor, 1979.
Leslie McManus, OPERATION BACKLASH, Playboy, 1979.
Clifford Mason, WHEN LOVE WAS NOT ENOUGH, Playboy, 1979.
Clyde Matthews, THE IDES OF MARCH CONSPIRACY, Playboy, 1981.
A.A. Miln, THE RED HOUSE MYSTERY, Dell Murder Ink, 1980.
Gladys Mitchell, WINKING AT THE BRIM, Dell Scene of the Crime, 1981.
Patricia Moyes, MANY DEADLY RETURNS, Dell Murder Ink, 1981.
James Munro, THE MONEY THAT MONEY CAN'T BUY, Charter, 1981.
James Munro, DIE RICH, DIE HAPPY, Charter, 1980.
Joseph Nathenson, RADNITZ, Manor, 1979.
Joseph Nathenson, SEE NAPLES AND DIE, Manor, 1979.
Russell O'Neil, VENOM, Ballantine, 1979.
Ruth Potts, NUGGET, Manor, 1979.
Raphael Rothstein, THE HAND OF FATIMA, Manor, 1979.
Peter Lars Sandberg, KING'S POINT, Playboy, 1979.
Jory Sherman, CHILL #6: HOUSE OF SCORPIONS, Pinnacle, 1980.

Patrick D. Smith, ALLAPATTAH, Manor, 1979.
Josephine Tey, A SHILLING FOR CANDLES, Pocket, 1980.
Trevanian, SHIBUMI, Ballantine, 1980.

OLDER HARDCOVERS, DESCRIBED AND PRICED INDIVIDUALLY:
John Buchan, THE COURTS OF THE MORNING, Houghton, Mifflin, 1929, g/vg, $3.
Miles Burton, THE HARDWAY DIAMONDS MYSTERY, Mystery League, 1930, first
    edition, good/vg, $4.00.
James Corbett, THE MERRIVALE MYSTERY, Mystery League, 1931, first edition,
    good, in tattered dj, $2.50.
Moray Dalton, THE BODY IN THE ROAD, Harper, 1930, first edition, ex-lib,
    water-damaged, worm-eaten, but intact, $1.00.
J.S. Fletcher, THE HARVEST MOON, Doran, 1927, slightly stained front
    cover, o/w good, $2.00.
_____, MURDER OF THE LAWYER'S CLERK, Knopf, 1st US, 1933, good, $2.00
Sydney Horler, PERIL, Mystery League, 1930, first edition, wear on top of
    front cover, sl. water damage, o/w good, $1.50.
A.E.W. Mason, THE FOUR CORNERS OF THE WORLD, Scribner's, 1917, g+, $3.00.
_____, THE PRISONER IN THE OPAL, Crime Club, 1928, 1st, vg, $4.00.
E. Phillips Oppenheim, THE INEVITABLE MILLIONAIRE, Little, Brown, 1925,
    good/vg, $2.50.
Eden Phillpotts, THE RED REDMAYNES, Macmillan, 1922, first? good+, $2.50.
Elmer L. Reizenstein, ON TRIAL, Dodd, Mead, 1915, first?, good/vg, with
    slightly worn and torn dj, $3.00.
Arthur Train, MCALLISTER AND HIS DOUBLE, Scribner's, 1905, first?, good/
    very good, $5.00.

OTHER HARDCOVERS, DESCRIBED INDIVIDUALLY, PRICED AT $2.00 EACH:
Charlotte Armstrong, A DRAM OF POISON, Coward-McCann, 1956, 2nd imp, good.
Francis Clifford, AMIGO, AMIGO, Coward, McCann & Geoghegan, 1973, first
    American edition, vg in good dj.
Joseph F. Dinneen, THE ANATOMY OF A CRIME, Scribner's, 1954, first, good.
Clive Egleton, SKIRMISH, Coward, McCann & Geoghegan, 1975, 1st US, vg in
    good dj.
Bruno Fischer, THE EVIL DAYS, Random House, 1973, 1st, vg in good dj.
Dick Francis, ENQUIRY, Harper [1970], 1st US, ex-lib, taped-on dj, o/w vg.
_____, FLYING FINISH, Harper [1967], 1st US, ex-lib, taped-on dj, o/w vg.
Brian Freemantle, HERE COMES CHARLIE M, Doubleday, 1978, 1st US, fine in
    vg dj (slight tear on front of dj).
Bernard Frizell, THE GRAND DEFIANCE, Morrow, 1972, near fine in vg dj.
Kyle Hunt, A PERIOD OF EVIL, World, 1971, 1st US, 1st prtg, vg in good dj.
Paul Jefferson, THE CUBAN HEEL, Macmillan, 1969, 1st prtg, vg in good dj.
John D. MacDonald, THE GIRL IN THE PLAIN BROWN WRAPPER, Lippincott, 1973,
    vg in good dj.
Helen MacInnes, ASSIGNMENT IN BRITTANY, Sun Dial Press, 1943, good+.
_____, THE DOUBLE IMAGE, Harcourt, Brace & World, 1966, 1st, vg in sld dj.
_____, THE SALZBURG CONNECTION, Harcourt, Brace & World, 1968, 1st, vg in
    good dj.
Oscar Millard, A MISSING PERSON, McKay-Washburn, 1972, fine in vg dj.
Paul Ørum, NOTHING BUT THE TRUTH, Pantheon, 1976, 1st US fine in vg+ dj.
Georges Simenon, MAIGRET SETS A TRAP, HBJ, 1972, fine in vg dj.
Alan White, THE LONG WATCH, HBJ, 1971, 1st US, vg+ in vg dj.
Andrew York, THE CAPTIVATOR, Doubleday/Crime Club, 1974, fine in good dj.

OLDER PAPERBACKS, DESCRIBED INDIVIDUALLY, PRICED AT $1.00 EACH:
Stuart Brock, KILLER'S CHOICE, Graphic 136, 1956, vg.
Leslie Charteris, THE SAINT IN ACTION, Avon 463, [1952], good.
Agatha Christie, PERIL AT END HOUSE, Pocket 167, Feb. '43, 4th prtg, good.
Mignon G. Eberhart, THE MAN NEXT DOOR, Dell mapback 161, loose cover ow g.

Erle Stanley Gardner, TCOT DUBIOUS BRIDEGROOM, Pocket C-376, October 1959,
    first printing, vg.
_____, TCOT BURIED CLOCK, Pocket 678, Feb 1950, 1st printing, vg+
_____, TCOT CARELESS KITTEN, Pocket 724, March 1952, 4th prtg, good-.
_____, TCOT CAUTIOUS COQUETTE, Pocket C-332, Nov'59, 2nd prtg, good.
_____, TCOT DUPLICATE DAUGHTER, Pocket 4504, June 1962, 1st prtg, good.
_____, TCOT FUGITIVE NURSE, Pocket 1138, Dec 1956, 1st prtg, good.
_____, TCOT GLAMOROUS GHOST, Pocket, C-282, Nov 57, 1st prtg, vg.
_____, TCOT HESITANT HOSTESS, Pocket C-381, Nov 1959, 1st prtg, vg.
_____, TCOT HOWLING DOG, Pocket 116, October 1945, 19th prtg, vg.
_____, TCOT LAZY LOVER, Pocket C-285, March 1958, 1st prtg, good-.
_____, TCOT LUCKY LOSER, Pocket C-341, June 1959, 1st prtg, good +.
_____, TCOT PERJURED PARROT, Pocket C-379, November 1958, 1st prtg, good.
_____, TCOT TERRIFIED TYPIST, Pocket C-275, August 1958, 1st prtg, good.
Dashiell Hammett, THE GLASS KEY, Dell 2915, July 1966, 1st prtg, good.
Matthew Head, THE CABINDA AFFAIR, Dell mapback 390, [1950], good.
Dorothy B. Hughes, DREAD JOURNEY, Pocket 454, Sept 47, 1st prtg, good +.
Francis Iles, BEFORE THE FACT, Pocket 419, March 1947, 1st prtg, vg+.
Hilda Lawrence, THE HOUSE, Avon PN387, September 1971, 1st prtg, good+.
Frances and Richard Lockridge, DEATH OF A TALL MAN, Dell mapback 322,
    [1949], good-.
Jerome Odlum, THE MIRABILIS DIAMOND, Dell mapback 303, [1949], good/vg.
Richard S. Prather, DEAD HEAT, Pocket 4801, Dec 1963, 1st printing, vg.
Ellery Queen, THE TRAGEDY OF Y, Pocket 313, August 1943, 1st prtg, good-.
H.W. Roden, TOO BUSY TO DIE, Dell mapback 185, [1947], vg.
Mickey Spillane, THE LONG WAIT, Signet 932, May 1952, 1st prtg, good/vg.

READING COPY PAPERBACKS, ALL INTACT, CONDITION GENERALLY GOOD, 50¢ EACH:
Edward S. Aarons, ASSIGNMENT: BUDAPEST, Fawcett R2040; ASSIGNMENT: THE
    GIRL IN THE GONDOLA, Fawcett, R2054; ASSIGNMENT: MANCHURIAN DOLL,
    Fawcett d1778; ASSIGNMENT: STELLA MARNI, Fawcett d1729.
Eric Ambler, JUDGMENT ON DELTCHEV, Bantam H3165.
Charlotte Armstrong, LEMON IN THE BASKET, Fawcett R1198.
George Harmon Coxe, DEATH AT THE ISTHMUS, Popular 60-2460.
Clive Egleton, THE BORMANN BRIEF, Fawcett P2480.
A.A. Fair, BATS FLY AT DUSK, Dell D348.
Ian Fleming, LIVE AND LET DIE, Pan X233; THE MAN WITH THE GOLDEN GUN,
    Signet P2735.
Erle Stanley Gardner, TCOT BURIED CLOCK, Pocket, 75522; TCOT COUNTERFEIT
    EYE, Pocket 50306; TCOT DARING DECOY, Pocket 4518; TCOT DEMURE DEFEN-
    DANT, Pocket C-323; TCOT DROWNING DUCK, Pocket, 50320; TCOT DROWSY
    MOSQUITO, Pocket 50323; TCOT FUGITIVE NURSE, Pocket 50343; TCOT GILDED
    LILY, Pocket 50351; TCOT ROLLING BONES, Pocket 50315; TCOT SILENT
    PARTNER, Pocket 4506; TCOT SMOKING CHIMNEY, Pocket 6014; TCOT STUT-
    TERING BISHOP, Pocket 50309; TCOT SUN BATHER'S DIARY, Pocket 4514;
    TCOT TERRIFIED TYPIST, Pocket 50349.
Adam Hall, THE QUILLER MEMORANDUM, Pyramid T-1274.
Donald Hamilton, THE BETRAYERS, Fawcett d1736; THE SILENCERS, Fawcett
    T2374; ditto, Fawcett d1641; THE WRECKING CREW, Fawcett d1646.
Cornelius Hirschberg, FLORENTINE FINISH, Avon PN 221.
Emma Lathen, DEATH SHALL OVERCOME, Pocket 77782.
Ross MacDonald [sic], HARPER [THE MOVING TARGET], Pocket 50218.
Ngaio Marsh, DEATH OF A PEER, Jove Y5413.
Richard S. Prather, TOO MANY CROOKS, Fawcett 551.
Ellery Queen, THE DOOR BETWEEN, Signet T4614.
Mickey Spillane, I, THE JURY, Signet 699; ditto, Signet P3382; KISS ME,
    DEADLY, Signet 1000; ditto, Signet P3270; THE LONG WAIT, Signet 932;
    ditto, Signet D2112; MY GUN IS QUICK, Signet 791; THE SNAKE, Signet,
    D2548; ditto, Signet Q5702; THE TWISTED THING, Signet D2949; VEN-
    GEANCE IS MINE, Signet 852; ditto, Signet D2116.

I say this even though I'd have to say I thought the plot of
the actual perpetrator to have been the least likely one of
them all. Cleverly done. (B plus)* (*Reviews so marked have
appeared earlier in the Hartford *Courant*.)

Stephen Greenleaf. *Grave Error*. Dial Press, 1979, 264 pp.

This book seems to have been published in a vacuum. I
don't really recall any fanfare or critical attention being
paid to it when it was published at all. Or if there was, I
missed it. And it's a shame, for it's certainly a book worth
the reading, especially if you're a private eye fan and don't
yet mind another tale of tangled Californian bloodlines.
The jacket says Greenleaf is a Chandler fan. It's easy to
believe. He must also be a devoted reader of Ross Macdonald.
The similes and other metaphorical flights of fancy are off
and soaring from the start. Or take it from page seven: "She
filled her blue knit dress the way a miser fills his coffers.
. . . The tiny gold turtle pinned over her left breast was as
smug as Governor Brown."
Greenleaf's detective is John Marshall Tanner, once a lawyer and now a private investigator. In this case it seems
that San Francisco has its own consumer-advocate version of
Ralph Nader, but Tanner is hired by the man's wife to investigate his strange recent behavior.
The pair also have an adopted daughter, and she has a
problem as well. This one results in the death of one of Tanner's closest friends, also a private eye.
I mentioned bloodlines. The trail of too many people
leads back to the small town of Oxtail, where too many secrets
have never been buried. I had half the answers right away,
and the half I didn't have explained why I didn't believe the
half I knew.
(It's not mathematically possible, I know, at least not in
the strict sense, but there is at least another twist and a
half before Tanner uncovers the full answer and a half.)
Keep an eye on Greenleaf. I believe he has a future. (B)

John D. MacDonald. *Free Fall in Crimson*. Harper & Row, 1981,
    246 pp., $10.95.

I've been doing some research. The first Travis McGee
story was entitled *The Deep Blue Goodbye*, and it was published
first as a paperback in May of 1964, back when a book sold in
soft cover would set you back all of forty cents or so.
It's now exactly seventeen years, eighteen books, and an
equal number of colors later, and real money, the folding
kind, is going to be what it takes to get your hands on a copy
of the latest in the series. No more loose pocket change!
This negative sort of progress notwithstanding, what this
does is to illustrate one of the most remarkable aspects of
John D. MacDonald's long writing career. Ignored by the critics until just recently, he began in the late 1940's writing
hundreds of stories published in the pulp magazines (and mostly still buried there). In the 1950's, with the demise of the
pulps at hand, he switched to novels, with a list of them
fully a page long, but all of them in paperback and in paper-

back only. Only in the last five or ten years has it been
that his books have come out first in hardcover, and now when
they do, they head straight for the bestseller list.

Readers have known all along. They've known that Mac-
Donald's name on a story has meant just what they've been
looking for.

Today, of course, MacDonald is best known for his adventures of Travis McGee. Other than myriads of articles for TV
Guide and blurbs for the dust jackets for the books of other
authors, he seems to be writing nothing else. It seems a
little strange for thos of us who've been with him all the
while, but apparently McGee is enough to keep the demands of
the vast majority of his legions of fans satisfied.

The format is restricting, but given the continued story-
telling drive of a *Free Fall in Crimson*, plus the usual amount
of free-wheeling MacDonaldian philosophy thrown in for good
measure, it seems unlikely that any change is due in the near
future.

In the opening chapters, McGee is still mourning the loss
of Gretel, lost but then avenged when last we met him, in *The
Green Ripper*. He is doing a lot of thinking about "destiny,"
and not until this new case comes along does he extricate himself from the deep, self-induced funk he's dug himself into.

He is asked to investigate, long after the fact, the
strange death of an artist's estranged father. The man was
dying of cancer, but perhaps not fast enough, for before he
does, he is beaten to death by persons unknown in an isolated
wayside rest area. His heir is his wife, from whom he was
legally separated. Her current boyfriend specializes in making R-rated biker movies, but his latest films have not been
faring well.

McGee's solution, when it comes to it, as it always does,
is to give fate a handy shove in the right direction. Fate's
response, as is usual in JDM's books, is tough and uncaring.
Unfortunately, McGee neglects some loose ends this time, and
as a result, in the next book it will be his best friend,
Meyer, who will need some rehabilitating.

In the Travis McGee universerse, it is not wise to stand
too close to the target area. (A minus)*

Arthur Lyons. *Hard Trade*. Holt, Rinehart & Winston, 1981,
253 pp., $10.95.

There must be more private eyes per capita in California
than anywhere else in the world. Jacob Asch is another one.
He's been around for a while, but he's never gotten himself so
deeply caught up in the muck and mire or foul-smelling poli-
tics as he does in this one.

Throughout their long celebrated history, the majority of
the work that private detectives do has been to deal with the
likes of blackmailers, errant spouses, and runaway daughters.
Common everyday problems like that. People like Jacob Asch
just don't end up on the county payroll, working for the leading maverick on the L.A. Board of Supervisors, or at least not
ordinarily.

While, on the other hand, private eyes *are* known for
fighting the system, they've almost always been loners, at
least in fiction, with hardly ever any kind of power or

authority behind them. Nor do they usually end up uncovering
a trail of corruption, tinged with illicit homosexual diver-
sions, leading up anywhere nearly as high as this--clear to
Sacramento and the governor's mansion.

This is heady atmosphere, there's no denying it, but what
it does mean, as whenever a story takes this route, is that
there's a lot less action involved, and the paperwork outweighs
the legwork by far. Have no fear, though--the ending is as
authentically sour as anything you can find in the works of
Chandler, say, and it does compensate a great deal for a
slower-than-usual course of events from Mr. Lyons.

There is, by the way, one other note that is safe to add.
Here is a book that Jerry Brown will definitely *not* be pleased
with. (B minus)*

A.S. Fleischman. *Danger in Paradise*. Gold Medal, 1953, 160 pp.

It's easily said, but the fact of the matter is that they
just don't write books like this any more.

Adventure thrillers, that is, written for the fun of it,
and for the reader's pleasure as well, without the bloated
look of a book aimed straight for the bestseller list.

Jefferson Cape is in a small village in Bali when a beautiful girl slips him a message. Upon his return to the United
States, she tells him, he is to make sure it is immediately
turned over to the CIA. Unfortunately, he is forced to miss
his boat, whereupon he distinctly finds himself a center of
attention, and from all sides.

He soon finds he has fallen in love with the girl, of
course, has doubts, has doubts erased, then raised again.
Underlying his every action, however, is a sense of honor and
chivalry no longer adhered to today, not even by the good guys.

Maybe you can just chalk this one up to nostalgia. (B plus)

F.U. Ashford. *A Packet of Trouble*. Robert Hale, 1971, 188 pp.

Or did I speak too soon?

There is a great deal of similarity between this much more
recent book and the last, too much so to say that whatever
tradition it represents is dead completely.

Jake Standish, for a lark, agrees to take a small package,
contents unknown, to Innsbruck from England, for a stamp
dealer named Gostoli.

There are third parties involved, of course, not all of
them on the same side, but all of them with the mysterious
contents of the package in mind. And there is a girl, and
she is not as innocent as she would have him believe. She
is playing some complicated game with him, and he knows it,
but he falls in love with her anyway.

This exciting trans-European auto tour is jam-packed with
close encounters and narrow escapes. In style, it is mose
reminiscent of a Manning Coles adventure, crossed with an
Eric Ambler, perhaps. There is nothing here that a smoothly
sophisticated Helen MacInnes could ever possibly produce.

But while the result is wholly predictable by any stan-
dards, and is burbling throughout with complete implausibili-
ties--you guessed it--this is the kind of book that still

manages to be a huge amount of fun to read.
And nothing more.
Or less. (C plus)

Barry Fantoni. *Mike Dime*. Franklin Watts, 1980, 198 pp.,
$9.95.

In 1948 the two leading detective pulp fiction magazines
were *Black Mask* and *Dime Detective Magazine*, probably in that
order, Neither, alas, is around today, but *Black Mask* it was
which provided the birthplace and main stomping ground for all
the great private detective heroes of the 1920's and 1930's.
And from *Dime Detective* comes the name of Barry Fantoni's new
detective hero, Mike Dime, and he's a private eye. What else?
In *Mike Dime* the book, Fantoni does his best to recreate
the world and atmosphere of the year 1948. The city is Phil-
adelphia, and Harry Truman has just pulled off his surprising
upset victory over Tom Dewey.
But 1948 was a long while after Dashiell Hammett had quit
writing, and Raymond Chandler had long since been swallowed up
by Hollywood. In their wake, all the wise-cracking imitators
had taken over, and Mike Dime manages to place no higher than
in the midst of these, most of whom--anybody remember Rex
McBride?--are forgotten today.
It's not that Barry Fantoni hails from England. He has the local
lingo down pat, and historically all his people and places are
exactly right. Dime, who is hired first to protect a bagful
of money and then to help a girl with a blackmailer problem,
is grubby but honest. His greatest problem is rather that, as
Fantoni attempts to develop a sense of the comedic as well as
the dramatic, in what are obviously intended to be the lighter
moments, the result, twice at least, is outrageously silly
slapstick instead.
It's fun to read, in a way, but unfortunately what it also
does is to remind us that this is the sort of private eye
caper which is nothing more than a make-believe fairy tale,
with beautiful women falling willy-nilly, for example, all
over the feet of the invincible hero, who comes complete with
dirty socks and a three-day old beard.
It is the story of a dream, a fantasy, one that doesn't
exist, and as Fantoni inadvertantly reminds us, except in the
world of fiction, it never really did.
This book has its heart in the right spot, but its world
is built upon a faulty foundation. (C)*

Nat Easton. *A Book for Banning*. Boardman/British Bloodhound,
1959, 189 pp.

Bill Banning is so successful as a writer of crime fiction
that he can be taken for a doctor by the Bently he drives. He
also, on the side, owns and operates a private detective agency,
complete with a small staff of amateur, but dedicated, oper-
atives.
In this, his fifth adventure, he's hired by a worried
aristocrat to find a book that's mysteriously disappeared,
claimed to contain forbidden official secrets. The man, as
Banning quickly discovers, also has a nymphomaniac for a wife,
and a pair of spoiled, but married, daughters.

Banning is not the brightest detective in the world. His secretary-assistant, Josie, seems to have the sharpest mind in the firm. Banning is also--how should I put this?--woman hungry. Sex starved.

This is all pretty much tolerable, but the last couple of chapters are mucked up something awful. The killer is fairly obvious, but the "book" is impossibly found in the wrong apartment, and the interview leading into the final summing up is badly set up.

Or was I just asleep already? (C minus)

Len Deighton. *XPD*. Alfred Knopf, 1981, 339 pp., $12.95.

Speaking of movies, this is going to be a good one.

Stories about World War II, and about the Nazis, and with lots of killing and loads of intrigue--sure fire box-office. And nothing less than Winston Chirchill's reputation is at stake in this one.

Here it is, four decades later. Len Deighton's somber re-citation of events may lack a li-tle something in the way of providing the sheer joy of reading that good writing is cap-able of, but in solid-documentary-like fashion, his main the-sis is nothing but convincing.

At least, it could have happened. In 1941, Churchill could have gone to Germany, hat in hand. He could have off-ered Hitler concessions in Africa and around the world. To end the war, he could have offered the Nazis joint control of Ireland. Is it fact, or fiction?

If it were true, emphasis on the if, it would certainly be embarrassing if it were to be found out today. It's no wonder the secret organizations of at least three countries--no, make it four--desperately want to locate the evidence. In the wrong hands, it would shake the world.

The movie that will be made from the book will probably be mostly flash, with little substance. Deighton's dry, almost academic style, complete with occasional footnotes, has always seemed just the reverse to me. The action comes in spurts, nor, strangely enough, does it really seem to provide the main thrust of the story.

You can easily end up reading this almost solely for the characters involved: the British agent whose divorced wife is the daughter of the director general of MI6 and his immediate superior; the Jewish ex-soldier who accidentally stole the documents in question from Hitler's secret cave, today a suc-cessful California businessman whose son is falling for the daughter of an ex-Nazi guard now in the movie business; and that ex-Nazi's superior, the spy who plays it three ways against the middle.

The relationships are all a tangle, as you can plainly see. Everyone who enters this world of shadows and sudden violence falls at once into a boggy quagmire of manipulation.

But, then, that's what you expect from a Len Deighton spy thriller, and that's what you get.

What else can I say, other than he's done it again? (B minus)*

Verdicts
(More Reviews)

Jon L. Breen. *What About Murder? A Guide to Books About Mystery and Detective Fiction.* Scarecrow Press, 1981, 157 pp., $10.00.

A friend remarked to me the other day that he felt we were living in another "Golden Age" of crime fiction. Had he been speaking of books *about* crime fiction he would have been more right.
In the last several years, we have had a deluge of such books, and how and where to spend one's money has been a hard question. But no longer, thanks to Mr. Breen's book.
In the last ten years, four indispensable works for the serious reader/collector of crime fiction have been published: *Twentieth Century Crime and Mystery Writers, The Bibliography of Crime Fiction, Enclyclopdia of Mystery and Detection,* and *A Catalogue of Crime.* To this list must now be added *What About Murder?*
From the charming introduction to the very complete index, this is a masterwork. I can do no better than to quote from the foreword by Ellery Queen: "It is a landmark in the field of books about mysteries--a brilliant, necessary, long-overdue reference work, written with charm and authority." As usual Ellery Queen expresses it much better than I could.
My only quibble is that in the introduction Mr. Breen states that he had to eliminate certain categories of works from consideration, including the literature on Sherlock Holmes, most works on films, and works on authors "who have made a significant contribution to literature *outside* the mystery field." The reason for my quibble is that the annotations are so insightful for the books that he does list, that one wishes he could have included more works.
As a bonus, in his introduction Breen points out what he feels are the gaps in the literature, including the lack of book-length works on John Dickson Carr, Mickey Spillane, Eric Ambler, and Cornell Woolrich (which gap Mike Nevins will fill one day). This is a marvelous book and should not on any account be passed up. Order it immediately if not sooner! (Steve Stilwell)

Robert Champigny. *What Will Have Happened: A Philosophical and Technical Essay on Mystery Stories.* Indiana University Press, 1977, 183 pp.

Robert Champigny is a research professor of French at Indiana University and has published extensively, in both French and English, as a literary critic, philosopher, poet, and novelist. In this often difficult study of mystery fiction, Professor Champigny applies some of the technical principles he developed in an earlier book, *Ontology of the Narrative,* to mystery stories.

The main body of the essay is divided into three sections: Mystery, Story, and Cryptogram. In the prologue and in "Mystery," he establishes boundaries for the mystery which he defines as a hermeneutic tale, a narrative in which "the goal and result of the narrative process is the determination of some events anterior to the ending of the process." "Mystery stories," he maintains in a statement which provides him with the title of his book, "sharpen the interest not just for what will happen but what will have happened." This compelling thrust of the narrative toward a future that will clarify events that may precede the novel's beginning also provides Professor Champigny with a justification of his violation of one of the rules which mystery reviewers, if not critics, have usually followed, the refusal to reveal the nature of the dénouement. Since he sees the structure as benefitting from the tension created by a narrative which continually moves both forward and backward, the dénoument is a primary technical pivot and a discussion of its forms and content a necessity in any analysis of the self-contained esthetic unit.

His belief in the esthetic integrity of the mystery novel also rises out of a sense that those novels are most satisfying where there is a transfiguring dénoument which, among several possibilities, appears to be most appropriate. This intuitive appreciation of a definitive ending--also suggested by the careful use of the future perfect in the essay's title-- leads him, in his opening chapter, to reject from a strictly defined canon those novels which "attract the reader's attention to some undetermined events but avoid determining them at the end." This may strike some readers as too confining a definition, but Professor Champigny only excludes unresolved mysteries from his canon, not from his discussion. In the third part of his essay, he comments at some length on "pseudo-narratives" of writers like Alain Robbe-Grillet and Michel Butor in which a narrative illness is described but not cured. As concerned as Professor Champigny professes himself to be about the closed ending, I find it ironic that he opens out his own descriptive narrative toward the end to include what he initially claims he is excluding. Thus he emphasizes the importance of the use of the techniques of mystery fiction by avant-garde writers who subvert them to their own ends. If a hermeneutic tale resolves its internal delimma, the pseudo-narrative does not, and works both against the processes of the genre and the esthetic pleasure which a reader like Professor Champigny normally derives from it.

What may be of particular interest in this discussion to American readers is his identification of Joel Townsley Rogers' novel *The Red Right Hand* as a forerunner of these experimental fictions. As he returns repeatedly to comment on this novel throughout his essay, Professor Champigny acknowledges the faithful adherence by Rogers to the principle of the resolved dénoument, but he also points out that much of the novel, in its apparent contradictions and multiple disguises, inhibits the investigative sequence leading to that dénouement.

Professor Champigny also discusses narrative viewpoint, the poetry of mystery fiction, the role of atmosphere, and the ambivalent relationship between the detective and the criminal, refering in detail to a number of continental as well as Anglo-American sources. *What Will Have Happened* is not for the casual reader of detective stories, and some sophisticated readers will be irritated by principles they see as soo confining. But popular genres are, in practice, restricted, and, to borrow a point from Professor Champigny, one can accept his reading of the genre without rejecting critical avenues that, in the hands of another critic, might produce conclusions that would be no less satisfying. (Walter Albert)

Margot Bennett. *The Man Who Didn't Fly*. Eyre & Spottiswoode, 1955, 191 pp.

A plane gets lost over the Irish Sea. Four people had arranged to go by the aeroplane on Friday morning. Only one of them was spared by chance, because he had failed to arrive at the airport. But instead of telling the world why he had missed the plane, he remains silent and invisible. Trouble is, we don't know which of them has stayed behind.

And then all the good fun begins. Just watch the police trying to find out about the identity of those who were on the plane. Listen to how they question Mr. Crewe, landlord in the pub at Brickford Airport, an old man with a disease of the liver, hating his wife and proving totally uncooperative. Or Mr. Murray, only loosely connected with one of the passengers, and yet feeling that whatever he will say, his interview with the police is not going to turn out well.

Flashbacks take us to the Wades (father and two daughters), who are acquainted with all the persons involved, two days before the fatal flight.

All the persons seem so real, and yet it's like a bad dream where you can't shout and interfere, just watch helplessly how people build their little private hells. But there's so much fun amidst all the scheming and malice, avarice and greed, unselfishness and readiness to help. Would any girl ever marry Harry, a poet, who is fond of playing Donegal Poker in the small hours? Is Uncle Joe a real friend of the family in distress, or is it business first? What about Morgan Price? Will he ever forget to send his Nanny a birthday card? Can Maurice stop worrying about his health? Have you ever met a genuine Australian rough-neck, or young Jackie, a reformed crook turned butler? And above all the Wades. Mr. Wade, forever trying to make some fast money, biggest fool on earth or loving father? Hester, romantic and compassionate girl in the good old sense of the word--and fifteen-year-old Prudence, most likeable of all the personae dramatis.

I was halfway through the book when the wish to have a look behind the facades and come to know the identity of the man who didn't fly and read the answers to all the riddles became almost too strong to resist. I had become part of the Wades' household, was angry with Hester's fool-hardy father and despised Harry for quoting poetry instead of making love, and suffered with Prudence, who would probably die if she couldn't tango perfectly by the end of the week.

Tension among the guests and visitors at the Wades' home

steadily grow throughout Thursday, the day before the flight;
and it culminates in a burst of violence that takes everyone
by surprise and yet acts as a kind of relief.

On Friday morning nothing is back to normal, but events
have at least taken their course. You are prepared for the
worst, but you don't mind; you have been through a lot; you
are tired, you have taken leave of those who must die; tris-
tesse has taken hold of you, you feel empty and dizzy like you
do the day after a party that has gone sour. It's all over
now. . . .

You should part with the book here, remembering Uncle Joe
and Hester and the rest of them, pleasant or unpleasant as
they are. And what about all the answers? Well, if that's
what you are after you could have looked them up some sixty
pages earlier. If it's the Wades and their acquaintances that
fascinate you, and the whirl of events they've been in, then
stop on Friday morning. But I'm sure you won't take my advice--
all right, you'll be in for something really bad. Suddenly
(and it's still some thirty pages to go) everything tastes
stale; the characters become cardboard; even the police lose
that threatening air of law enforcement and turn out to be a
couple of good-natured busybodies who--with their fingers
raised--hammer the truth into everyone who wants to know it.
Objects suddenly begin to matter--the number of roses in a
vase is more important than the way they may look on a corpse.
Lines from an opera have a significance unparalleled by anything that's been said so far. . . .

There are still a few good lines left, but they are no
compensation for brutes that go soft and girls that suddenly
know what true love is like.

Only one of the dead is strangely alive (. . . if only
in our memory). (Helmuth Masser)

John D. MacDonald. *Free Fall in Crimson*. Harper & Row, 1981,
246 pp., $10.95.

For millions of readers of crime fiction John D. MacDonald
is *the* consumate storyteller, who, with his energetic prose,
his vivid sense of character, his all but miraculous skill at
describing every sort of person and setting and event with
economy, elegance, and total credibility, makes us turn and
turn his pages with our minds in awe and our hearts hovering
around our Adam's apple. MacDonald came back from World War
II service in India and Ceylon with the itch to write, and he
supported himself for the next several years by turning out
millions of words--the best of them even then fantastically
good--for the pulp mystery and western and sports and science-
fiction magazines. In 1950 he published his first novel, not
in hardcover but as a paperback original, and continued to
write paperbacks so prolifically and well that he forced critics and intelligent readers to take notice of a medium they
might otherwise have dismissed as junk. In 1964, with the
debut of his series character, the philosophical boatbum-
adventurer Travis McGee, MacDonald's royalties and readership
soared even higher, and eventually author and hero migrated to
hardcover and to the bestseller lists. McGee's nineteenth and
latest exploit is already on the charts--and for good reason.

When a plastics tycoon dying of cancer is beaten to death

at a rest area off a Florida highway, his estranged artist son becomes convinced that the murder was part of a complex plot to channel the old man's estate into the hands of the victim's not yet divorced wife, and he prevails upon an action-starved McGee to reopen the case. The trail brings McGee back into the lives of several survivors of earlier adventures, such as actress Lysa Dean from *The Quick Red Fox* (1964) and propels him into the worlds of independent moviemakers and baloonists and outlaw motorcycle gangs along the road to the climactic encounter with another in MacDonald's gallery of psychotic butchers.

The nineteenth McGee may not be the best in the series-- the buildup is a bit slow and deliberate, the specialized knowledge sometimes to hypertechnical, and the climax jarring- ly abrupt--but it's a wonderful non-stop read, full of off- trail life styles and menace and relationships and philosophy and suspence, dominated as always by the aging, self-mocking, self-appointed contemporary knight who is perhaps the closest to a naturalistically credible hero figure the genre has pro- duced in the last twenty years. "We live in the flatlands and the myths are our mountains," McGee reflects, "so we build them to change the contours of our lives, to make them more interesting." The marvelous myth-world of John D. MacDonald, the world of knightly quests and adoring ladies and fearsome monsters rooted in the landscape of the way we live now, con- tinues after thirty-five years to make life more interesting for millions of readers. (Francis M. Nevins, Jr.)

John Dickson Carr. *Scandal at High Chimneys*. Harper, 1959.

When I read this book, it was one of the few John Dickson Carr titles that I had yet to read. Most of the Carr titles are straight detection with such detectives as Gideor Fell, Bencolin, etc. However, they often have spurious supernatural elements and sometimes comedy. Carr, of course, is the expert of the locked room mystery sub-genre. Many of Carr's other titles fall into the historical novel class in the sense that they have a setting in a period of British history some time prior to the twentieth century. Since *Scandal at High Chimneys* is subtitled, A Victorian Melodrama, I was sure into which class it fell.

Like many of Carr's tales, this one is narrated by an in- telligent young man--in this case Clive Strickland--who hap- pens to fall in love with one of the many suspects. This tale is unusual, however, in that it has an inverted locked room twist. By this I mean that the reader and the narrator know what has happened, but until the narrator's story is believed by the other characters, they are befuddled by what has hap- pened in the murder room. Even though the narrator (and the reader) knows what has happened, he does not know *who* is re- sponsible. The detective who is consulted is named Whicher; he is not now part of the official force because of something that happened years before. Whicher proves to be astute and brings the case to a successful conclusion.

I found the book more enjoyable than many of Carr's his- torical adventures. The mystery of who committed the crimes is just deep enough to keep one guessing. The clues are in sight if the reader digs a little bit. Also, there are ref- erences to such notables as Charles Dickens and Edmund Kean

which provide a pleasant diversion. Car, in "Notes for the
Curious," amply documents his references in this tale. All
in all, this book is worth seeking out. (Jeffery Koch)

Nicholas Blake. *The Dreadful Hollow*. Harper, 1953.

Nigle Strangeways is asked to investigate a series of
anonymous poison-pen letters in the remote English village of
Prior's Umborne. Upon arriving there, he finds that there are
deep, hidden undercurrents of sexual and religious repression.
Nigel quickly ingratiates himself with the local police and
discovers the author of the letters to his own satisfaction.
However, this is only the beginning, as a murder is committed
which seems to tie in with the letter-writing campaign. Nigel
must discover the murderer while at the same time sorting out
the hidden sexual and religious motivations. This he does
using his ideas of psychological motivation along with an
acute reading of psychological and physical clues. The clues
are available to the reader, who should be able to figure out
the identity of the murderer. Beware of a plot twist at the
end, however.
There is a true malevolence in this tale, which I found
somewhat unusual for a Strangeways story. The hidden currents
were also unusual, reminding me more of P.D. James or Ruth
Rendell. Yet, the story was handled with a lightness which
seems to mark a typical Strangeways story. This is definitely
the type of story that one wants to read through without
putting it down. (Jeffery Koch)

Lawrence Sanders. *The Secnod Deadly Sin*. Putnam, 1977.

Long, leisurely police procedural in which retired Chief
of Detectives Edward X. Delaney is pressed back into service
to investigate the brutal slaying of the acclaimed artist,
Victor Maitland. It is soon apparent that Maitland was suf-
ficiently outrageous to have potential killers standing in
line at the doorway, so that Delaney has quite a job on his
hands. What is more, he isn't always greatly helped by his
aide, Sergeant Abner Boone, an alcoholic desperately trying
to stay off the habit. But Delaney isn't a man who's easily
defeated, and he and Boone painstakingly sift through the
evidence, re-interview the suspects, and finally unmask the
killer. This is a nice long novel in which Sanders, a natural
storyteller, can take his time to develop his plot and breathe
life into his characters. It doesn't have that same sense of
the weird and the sinister that *The First Deadly Sin*(in which
Delaney also appeared) had, but it's nevertheless a first
class mystery novel. (Bob Adey)

Peter Van Greenaway. *A Man Called Scavener*. Gollancz, 1978.

Mystery novels set in cathedral closes are not exactly
thick on the ground (Gilbert's *Close Quarters*, of course), and
this book is certainly a most unusual and sometimes disturbing
novel. At least Alex Waterlow, a prodigal son if ever there
was one, finds the Scavener family, ensconsed in their antique

emporium, rather disturbing. Ascetic old man Scavener, his
shrew of a daughter Carry, the distinctly odd son Gerald, with
whom Waterlow was at school, and the always absent Edwina,
hideously disfigured (we are told) in a dreadful accident.
But how was Edwina disfigured, and why does Gerald take a
dangerously morbid interest in a nineteenth century murderer,
and just how did Alex's late uncle, a former partner in the
antiques business, come to die so suddenly? There's much of
the gothic in the unravelling of this skein of mystery, and I
was often reminded of Michael Innes. The writing has a dis-
tinctive flavour, and the whole book is quite out of the ordinary. (Bob Adey)

B. M. Gill. *Death Drop*. Hodder & Stoughton, 1979.

     A first crime novel and the most compulsive book I've read
for months. Widower John Fleming flies back at once from India when he learns that his twelve-year-old son, his only
child, has been killed in a fall. But the boy when found was
wearing a blindfold, and his father can't believe--won't be-
lieve--that it was the accident that the public school concerned says it was. The book follows his efforts to prove
that his son's death was due to something more sinister, and
it vividly describes his growing bitterness as he meets oppo-
sition at almost every turn. His only ally is the young
school matron, but it is finally through another person that
the truth emerges. Not particularly strong on detection, but
extremely good writing and characterisation--particularly of
Fleming, thwarted at every turn, and of the misfit schoolboy,
Durrant. I can guarantee that you will have considerable
difficulty in putting this one down.
     N.B.: English public schools are in fact all private, fee-
paying schools. (Bob Adey)

Sheila Radley. *The Chief Inspector's Daughter*. Scribner's,
     1980.

     Sheila Radley's *The Chief Inspector's Daughter* is almost
certainly her best novel to date. Chief Inspector Douglas
Quantrill and his second, Detective Sergeant Tait, investigate
the especially violent murder of Jasmine Woods, collector of
netsuke and jade and writer of vastly successful romantic
novels. There are troops of suspects, as almost all of the
wealthy writer's friends and relatives have reasons for covet-
ing her money or envying her success and her apparently secure,
comfortable way of life.
     The investigation is complicated and intensified by the
fact that Quantrill's daughter, Alison, who has taken a job as
secretary to Jasmine Woods, discovers the body and, suffering
from shock and grief, disappears. Alison certainly has information useful to the police and may well be in considerable
danger from the murderer. The teenager is troubled not only
by the murder but also by the after-effects of a failed love
affair.
     Naturally, Alison's parents are desperately worried about
her disappearance and concerned about her recovery from the
affair. And as always in the Quantrill novels, the difficult

relationship between Douglas and Molly is an important feature. In this story, both Quantrill and the reader come to understand Molly a little better, and the policeman's wife emerges as a fuller, somewhat more sympathetic, character.

The character of the slick, ambitious, libidinous Martin Tait is also more fully developed here. Tait has met Jasmine Woods a few months before her death and has found her to be extremely attractive, but Jasmine proves to be a worthy foil for the junior officer. On the other hand, the relationship between Quantrill and Tait seems to have shaken down into a more open, more cooperative alliance. The men are still a bit wary of one another, but each is capable of flashes of true (and not always comfortable) insight about his partner. This pattern makes for fine characterization and excites a good deal of interest.

Also interesting is the characterization of the victim. Jasmine Woods is a talented writer and a complete realist. She likes to live well and so writes the kind of novels which sell well--despite the scorn of the more "serious" writers in her circle. This factor allows radley to make some keen comments about romantic fiction, its appeal, and its possible effects on its readers, observations firmly wedded to the plot and the action.

Actually, the Radley-Woods comments on the romances are well-founded and well-taken, and they should be of special interest to readers of mystery-detective novels, for they can apply handily to that genre also. First of all, the point is made that there's nothing wrong with good, entertaining writing; after all, one of the main ends readers seek *is* entertainment. There's nothing wrong, either, with a little escapism, and Radley, through her fictional writer, points out that no author can *make* readers seek undue refuge in such works. Finally, the presence of good, taut narration, fast movement, and solid plots is stressed. Without pressing the point, Radley makes clear that Woods is a good writer who chooses, for perfectly good reasons, to write in a lucrative form. Two points underlie these comments, and though they are never voiced, they are apparent: (1) reading does *not* corrupt people or blind them to the true conditions of their lives, though it can serve to make those lives more bearable, and (2) a really good writer, like Woods, like Radley, embellishes her "light" fiction with saltings of serious thought (as here) and with good characterizations. All very true, and all neatly put.

Through Alison Quantrill, Jasmine Woods, and her close friend, Roz Elliott, a militant feminist, Radley also delivers herself of some comments about the Women's Movement. Roz condemns Jasmine for feeding unliberated women's escapist fantasies, but both friends realize that there are great ironies in their own life styles. Because Alison is at a crossroads in her own life, she examines the choices Jasmine's and Roz's patterns represent, as well as the extended family enjoyed by Polly, Roz's sister. These four women and Molly Quantrill make up a gallery of fine characterizations.

Radley's best creation, however, remains her protagonist, Douglas Quantrill. Dedicated and thoughtful, he sees not only the value and necessity of his work, but also the tragic impact of the crimes:

Quantrill felt neither anger nor triumph. He felt tired, dis-

pirited by the years he had spent in trying to clear up the dirt,
the follies and greeds and overflowing emotions, the sickness of
humanity. What saddened him most was that, ultimately, it was
not only the victims of murder who suffered but the innocents on
the periphery of every case: the ones who were left to manage as
best they could, the wives, the husbands, the children, the par-
ents, not only of the victim but of the criminal .

Though Quantrill does become tired and discouraged, he does
not become jaded, and neither do readers, largely because the
introspective hero can and does change, develop, and grow.
For all these sound reasons, *The Chief Inspector's Daughter* is
a fine novel. (Jane S. Bakerman)

Douglas Clark. *Roast Eggs*. Golancz, 1981, 175 pp.

This is, by one count at any rate, the fifteenth book in
Douglas Clark's series about his team of Scotland Yard detectives, George Masters and William Green. Having started out
as Chief Inspector and Detective Sergeant, respectively, and
with a very thorny relationship, Masters and Green have by now
been promoted to Superintendent and Chief Inspector, and have
mellowed into a friendly and very effective investigative team.
It now appears that the present book and its two predeces-
sors (*Poacher's Bag* and *Golden Rain*) have been in a sense var-
iations on a theme: placing the Scotland Yard detectives in an
assortment of unusual situations in which they must not only
uncover the facts of a crime but exert their ingenuity to have
those facts placed officially on record within the sometimes
frustrating limits of the British judicial system.
In the case at hand, Masters and Green are called upon in
the final stages of a court trial. James Connal has been
charged with the murder of his wife (via arson); the prose-
cutor's case has already been completed and all witnesses have
testified. To conclude its presentation, the defense calls
Connal to testify on his own behalf--and he is doing such a
good job of it that the police case is being eroded and the
jury's sympathies swayed in his favor. The investigating officer and the prosecuting counsel are both convinced that Connal is guilty and equally convinced that he is likely to get
away with his crime. Masters and Green, given only a weekend
recess in which to work, and with only transcripts of the
trial rather than first-hand investigation to work with, have
first to convince themselves of Connal's guilt and then to
find some way of preventing the trial from ending in acquittal.
the account of their investigations occupies roughly the
middle third of the book. That the author manages to make
this actionless interlude compelling reading, and also con-
trives to save a surprise or two for the climactic courtroom
scene, are measures of his admirable cleverness and skill in
both plotting and prose. Not unexpectedly, the denouement
involves another of the bits of uncommon medical knowledge
which have become the author's hallmark.
Relatively few of Clark's books have been reprinted in the
U.S., and even in England the older titles are not easy to
find. But anyone who enjoys solid craftsmanship, intricate
plotting, and smooth writing will be more than rewarded by the
search. (R.E. Briney)

Mary McMullen. *The Other Shoe*. Doubleday/Crime Club, 1981.

Thunk goes the other shoe when it falls. And this latest
from McMullen represents a real fall from grace--thunking like
the heaviest hob-nailed brogan. It's not that this is a *terrible* book. The story is capable of holding reader interest.
One evening Justin Channon finds his long lost and lovely
cousin, Clare, on his doorstep. Four years earlier Clare had
been tried (and narrowly acquited) on the charge of murdering
her bitchy rich aunt. A threatening note brings her to Justin,
who vows to help her and eventually breaks the case and gets
the girl. McMullen's writing skills are solid enough to keep
this from being a real ho-hummer despite an ending I found
both abrupt and unsatisfying.

The biggest disappointment is, however, less the book itself than the realization it brought home to me. McMullen has
become yet another personal formula writer. She has found a
comfortable personal recipe for romantic mystery. The recipe
works, so she seems content using it over and over again.
Clare is like any number of earlier heroines. Lovely yet
brave, she dresses like a dream without being overly ostenta-
tious in her apparel. To show how modern she is, at least one
outfit consists of a silk shirt and a pair of slacks. You
can't, after all, spend all your time in dresses made out of
"chiffon handkerchiefs." Justine (like Jeremy, Augustus, and
other McMullen men with designer names) is strong, kind, and
beautiful to look at. He never seems to lose his air of
"freshly showered ease" and "graceful quiet authority." For
such perfect people, can there be any doubt that their trials
are crowned with triumphs--and happily-ever-afters?

It is unfair to pick on Mary McMullen, who is no worse
than hundreds of other authors. But such obvious plot and
character formularization is inexcusable in a writer of Mc-
Mullen's talent and lineage. Perhaps next time she'll cook
up something really new. For now, if you haven't read any
Mc-Mullen before, then *The Other Shoe* may provide an enjoyable
read. If you're a McMullen reader from way back, don't bother.
There's nothing new here. Go back and reread *A Country Kind
of Death, Funny, Jonas, You Don't Look Dead,* or even the more
recent *But Nellie Was So Nice*. The formula was fresher then.
It worked better. (Kathi Maio)

The Documents In the Case

(Letters)

From Joe L. Hensley, 2315 Blackmore St., Madison, IN 47250:
[*Joe was one of the mystery celebrities on this year's Mystery Cruise, and he passes on this account of the happenings:*] The boat left from Fort Lauderdale on April 18. It was a 19,500-ton cruise liner. When Char and I went aboard the first person we saw was Dilys. She introduced us to the Westlakes. Everyone went their own way and we met again at dinner, still tied to the dock. There we met the rest of the crew, John D. and Dorothy MacDonald, Chris Steinbrunner, Al Nussbaum, Marie Castoire and Mike Gatto (two New York police officers), and Ruth Windfeldt and her husband, Al. The food, as it was throughout the voyage, was quite good. Westlake and his wife, Abbie, are wine wise, so we drank well on white and red. Eventually the boat left and we stoon on deck and watched the people in condominiums winking their lights at us.

Along on the cruise were Clayton Matthews and his wife, Patricia, who do those huge saga love books (and do them very well), and they became a part of the crowd.

On the cruise we did two mystery whodunit plays where those in the audience had to figure out the killer. Near voyage end some of the passengers did one and we had to figure out the end. All great fun. We gave talks and Dilys put us into tandem combinations, one where Al Nussbaum and Marie and Mike and I wound up as the cop, robber, and judge. Chris cast and recorded a radio play from the golden years, "Cabin B-13," and it was very well done. A substantial number of people watched it live (with Dilys doing crazy ads at commercial times), and then it was later played over the ship's radio. There were special late night mystery movies, Don's "Cops and Robbers" and others.

We got to know everyone pretty well and liked them all. One of these days, up the line, I'm going to try to get Al N. to Indiana to talk to judges. He makes a lot of sense and does it very humorously. He's irreverent and irrepressible and I'd drive five hundred miles out of the way to see him again. The two New York police were splendid people, very street wise and interesting to listen to. They were nice to me when judges kept catching hell from their audiences.

Westlake is extremely funny in a small crowd. He knows many people I know. Asked about his work habits, he said this: "I hate slaving over a typewriter one day in a row."

John D. MacDonald comes over very gently. What he says

38

makes sense. He made two talks and I found myself hanging on
every word. He's been, for me, a sort of personal idol. The
publishers had sent books along, and he won one of mine (*A
Killing in Gold*) for a question. He read it and said some
nice things about it. When pressed, he also told me some
things which might be wrong (which is of far more value). His
wefe, Dorothy, was a lovely lady and they had two friends with
them, the Browns, who'd lived for a while in or near Louis-
ville (close to us), who were fun.
    We stopped at Bermuda, which looked great for golf. We
were then five days at sea before Funchal, Madeira. Char and
I found it fairly drab and not of any real interest, but we
heard the weather is very nice year round.
    At Tangiers we toured the Casbah with Marie and Mike, the
two N.Y. police officers. We walked miles with a native guide
who spoke better English than some people I see in court who've
lived here all their lives. The Casbah is dirty and it was
raining. People wanted to buy my cap. At Gibralter that
afternoon we toured with Mike and Marie in a cab. The apes
got on our cab at the top, perhaps recognizing me as a long
lost relative.
    The weather was bad leaving Gibralter, but calmed that
night late. Char took to bed, but I sat with John D. and the
Browns for a while at the costume ball.
    Barcelona was lovely and well-kept in the sun. Our guide
was proud of it, and we liked it and would like to go back for
a longer visit. Corsica, the next day, was very French and
also clean and lovely.
    The people at our table held a party the last night. That
was Don and Abbie, Mike and Marie, Al Nussbaum, Chris, and us.
John D. snapped portraits of most of us and autographed them,
we drank farewell toasts, and the next morning, after fifteen
days, it was over. Char and I went to Lucerne, Switzerland,
for a few days, someplace we'll go again, and then to Paris
where I had lunch with my French agent.
    One person I almost left out is Peter Carr. He's an Eng-
lish TV producer who does things for the BBC and was hand in
glove with us on several things, including one of the plays.
We exchanged addresses with him before he got off in Barcelona
and hope to see him again one day. Very sharp and talented.
    It was great to go, and I'm indebted to Dilys for inviting
me. Char doesn't handle rough water very well, so there goes
that barefoot cruise we were talking about. Next time we'll
fly, but I'm glad we went on this one.

From Bill Crider, 4206 Ninth Street, Brownwood, TX 76801:
    It may be that some of your more gullible readers were
fooled by your feeble complaint that there were not enough
letters to fill the most recent issue of TMF, but not me. I
know better. A quick glance through your letter section will
reveal to anyone that there is not a single letter in there
from anyone who has ever seen you in person. Those in the
know will realize that you suppressed all such letters because
every one made some comment about the accuracy of John McAleer's
statement of your resemblance to Audie Murphy. I can see that
you might not have had space for my own ten-page, point by
point analysis of just exactly how close your physiognomy ap-
proximates that of Murphy, but you should have printed at
least three or four of the other letters from those who have

seen you and who know just how right McAleer was. My own resemblance to Archie Goodwin is too well known by all your
readers to need any comment by me, of course; but we all know
that no matter how much you disagreed with Lee Horsley's in-
terpretation of Archie, you'll have to admit that the part
could never have been attempted by Audie Murphy. [*Bill, Bill,
Bill. You really must try to keep your delusions under control. I've been very patient with you, as I am sure everyone
will agree, but there are limits beyond which even a person as
good-hearted as I am cannot be pushed. My forbearance up to
this point has owed much to my well-known unwillingness to say
anything whatever that might in any way possibly offend any
person on earth, be he (or she, or it) living, dead, or somewhere in between. But if you persist in your pretense that
you look more like Archie Goodwin than I do, I will be forced
to make public the sordid details of how, at the Washington
Bouchercon, you tried to pass yourself off as Captain Midnight
to a partying flock of retired WAFs. I might even go so far
as to make public your unspeakable behavior with the Ovaltine,
although, this being a family publication, I could never go
into the full details. So watch it.*]
   And speaking of Archie, Marv Lachman's Wolfe article
wasn't bad; frankly, I'd never thought of Wolfe as President
myself, but Marv makes an ingenious case.
   I enjoyed Walter Albert's expert dismemberment of the
Skene Melvin Bibliography almost as much as Walter must have
enjoyed writing it. His reference to the "syntactically
bizarre" semicolon was one of the highpoints of the issue.
That's a phrase I'm going to have to remember.
   Do you think Scribner's would accept a Nick Carter story?
[*Not from you, bud. You are, like Martin Wooster, now a pro.*]

From Robert Samoian, 11308 Yearling St., Cerritos, CA 90701:
   Congratulations to you on the improved format of TMF--the
cover art and the artwork for the various article headings are
appropriate for a journal of quality, which is what TMF is,
and there are very few typos. Which brings me to a possibly
trivial, but nevertheless interesting, subject of printed errors in the spelling of author's names.
   In *The Case of the Curious Heel* by Ken Crossen, a digest-
sized paperback published as an Eerie Series publication in
1944, the author's name is correctly spelled on the cover, but
on the title page appears "by Ken Crosson."
   Lee Head's *The Crystal Clear Case*, Putnam, 1977, contains
the following dust jacket notation: "And in a scintillating
finale as reminiscent of James Bond as of Agathy Christy,
Lexey Jane meets her enemies head-on--and has to escape before
she is killed in her own trap."
   Putnam again, in 1979, is guilty of an error in *The Demon
Device*, by Sir Arthur Conan Doyle as communicated to Robert
Saffron, wherein there is a credit on the copyright page to a
quotation form John Dickson Carr's *Life of Sir Arthur Conan
Doyle*. While on page 11 Carr's name is correctly spelled, on
the copyright page it appears twice as "John Dicksun Carr."
   Can any TMF readers provide other examples of such errors?
If Agatha could be so wronged, perhaps there exists errata of
the likes of Karr, Sayres, Queer, Steet, Coile, and, heaven
forbid, Po?

From Steve Stilwell, 3425 Nicollet Ave. Minneapolis, MN 55409:
A number of things were enjoyable and interesting in the
last issue of TMF (5/5), but the most intriguing was Mr. Van
Tilburg's letter in which he mentions hardback books about Sam
Durell. This fact not sounding familiar, and my bibliographic
interest being activated, I opened *The Bibliography of Crime
Fiction* and found no listing of hardcover Durell titles there
either. Did Gold Medal do some hardcover publishing or were
there some titles published only in England in hardcover that
Al Hubin didn't know about? Perhaps Mr. Van Tilburg would
provide us with the information, before the future Durell
dossier.
Reading Walter Albert's critique of the Skene Melvin bibliography made me pleased that he didn't choose to do that
close a study of my TAD index. His points were all well taken,
and the fact that an index to TAD appears to have been in exis-
tance for at least part of the time that their work was in
progress makes the omission of that information even more inexcusable. Especially for a work that is called comprehensive
by the compilers.
For Linda Toole: the best edition of "Drood," or at least
the one I would recommend, is the Heritage Press edition with
introduction and notes by Vincent Starrett. Out of print, but
it should be available in used bookstores.

From Linda Toole, 147 Somershire Dr. Rochester, NY 14617:
No fair, Guy--telling us there are errors in the Stout
bibliography and then not enumerating them. Perhaps there
will be a sheet of errata? [*The errors are mostly typos,
though I know most of you will find that quite hard to believe;
so far as I know, there are no errors of fact.*]
I loved Marvin Lachman's article. [*Oh, you did, did you?
I thought it was plain outrageous, especially the part equat-
ing Wolfe with Nixon. But so highly developed is my noble
sense of editorial objectivity and fairness, that I used it
anyway. Everyone gets his say in TMF--even madmen like Lachman.*] Since Rex Stout is no longer with us, it would be interesting to get John McAleer's opinion. Personally, I think
of Wolfe more as Holy Roman Emperor or God, not a mere President!
I'm lifting the following information from TPP, and I hope
Jeff Meyerson won't mind. Gary Niebuhr is asking for reactions to the idea of an amateur mystery fiction magazine. He
envisions fifty to a hundred pages, three-fourths fiction, one
quarter l.o.c.s. Please send your reactions to Gary Niebuhr,
1521 S. 75th St., West Allis, WI 53214.
I'm hoping someone can help me out with some information
about Collier's "Front Page Mystery" series--how issued, how
many books, titles, etc. I recently came across one in a used
book store and couldn't resist. The one I have has a black
simulated leather cover with pictures of various murder wea-
pons (rifle, noose, poison, ect.) embossed on the front cover.
The title page says it is the "fifth series." Any light that
could be shed would be appreciated.

From Jeff Banks, Box 13007 SFA Sta. Nacogdoches, TX 75962:
Beware! Your latest (5:3) has provoked a second Banks
letter in a single year! [*Gasp!*] Maybe there's something to
that idea of yours that I should have my head examined. As

with writing you something more substantial, I simply don't
have time for that right now.

Thanks for keeping us posted on things like the Scribner
contest; I've a P.I. novel making the rounds now that I'll enter if I can't sell it to someone else by midsummer. Bleiler's
expected antiquarianism was as interested as Dueren's unex-
pected. Both these guys are fine writers you should persuade
to contribute more offten than you have in the past. Dawson
on le Carre, the written version of a paper presented at the
April national meeting of the Popular Culture Association, de-
served to be printed; let me publicly apologize for delaying
his joining the ranks of TMF subbers. *Mea clupa!* I'm sure he
will cook up something else on some spy writer soon for you.

Speaking of spies, I continue to enjoy Barry Van T's dos-
siers. But I can't help wondering why he excludes the paperback originals. Atlee and Hamilton, and some other fine writers who are head and shoulders (or, in the vernacular, mole
and cyphers) above many of those he *has* written about, are
thus unfairly overlooked.

Lachman's column, almost always (as this time) about facts
I already knew, but presenting them in an intriguingly new
configuration, continues to seem better and better to me.

As usual, I won't comment on the letter section, except to
say that one of the nicest features of your headlong rush to
catch up with your schedule has been the curtailment of the
letters. On, then, to what TMF is really all about--REVIEWS.

Steve's column continues to be my favorite item in each
issue. By now I understand very well where his and my tastes
overlap (not often) and conflict; I appreciate the meatiness
of his reviews. Often the books he waxes most enthusiastic
about are the ones that I intend to know only through his reviews, and I feel he helps me know them quite well enough.
Even when he pans a book I expect to like, he usually does so
cogently enough that I feel I know just what I'm going to enjoy the most. It's something like reading the bulletin board
in my army days: the list of OFF LIMITS premises usually told
me where the best fun was to be found.

Individual reviews: I agree wholeheartedly that Lathen
(even in a sub-par book) is still a good read, and I've had
the impression for the past couple of years that the quality
has fallen off a bit. On the other hand, that may just be the
result of too rapid consumption. After I made the inevitable
discovery (with the doctors book), I read about one a month
until I caught up. Could there be such a malady as Lathen
diabetes?

Crider's review of Lansdale's sleeper *Act of Love* (whose
original title was the much more appropriate *Let There Be
Blood*) seems right on target. If East Texas sales are anything to judge by (and if they were, your circulation would be
several million more than it is right now, I realize) then the
book may go into multiple printings.

By the way, Lansdale seems to have sparked something of a
Renaissance in Nacogdoches. Leaving aside my own writing
(which is two years old last month and, like most two-year-
olds, is still in the smelly diaper stage), lots of people
seem to be getting suddenly into the act. In the past couple
of months I have read a fine spy novel in rough draft, a probably unprintable but awfully interesting private eye novel
(no, not my own), and heard of another suspense novel and an

academic satire novel and a mainstream novel--all well along.
Lansdale can take a bow, or the blame, for most of that hap-
pening. Another protege of his, now living in Houston, had a
story in the May (or was it April?) *Mike Shayne.*
    The Vidoq and Burnett books I must make time (anybody know
how?) to read. Other reviews were interesting and mentioned
one or two other books that I probably will get around to
eventually.
    I'm looking forward to next month and an even shorter
letters section.

From Walter Albert, 7139 Meade St., Pittsburgh, PA 15208:
    I agree with Bleiler that the biographies and biblio-
graphies in Reilly's *Twentieth Century* are invaluable. I
wasn't aware that Reilly compiled all the bibliographies. And
read proof, too? If there is any justice, he will at least
get an Edgar for his work. [*He did.*]
    E.F. Bleiler wonders how he might get review copies of
European material. I would think that Iwan Hedman or Jacques
Baudou (of *Enigmatika*) might be able to advise him on that.
I've worked out an arrangement with Baudou in which we send
one another secondary works but we still pay at one end or the
other. In all the years I have been compiling the TAD bibliography I have been sent one reference work and that was the
Skene Melvin, whose review will probably ensure that I don't
receive any more. It is likely that European publishers send
out review copies to a list, and it might be possible to write
individual publishers and present onés case for the books.
    Unlike EFB, I hope that the academic writing controversy
does not open up any more. His comment that "some of your
people confuse scholarship with pedantry" is apt and really
says all that needs to be said on the subject. Let us hope
that we can all try to write well and informatively in a var-
iety of styles and modes.
    [*From a post script to another letter:*]
    I meant to mention in the letter I posted to you yesterday
that I enjoy Lachman's column. Entertaining notes, and I hope
he will keep writing them for you. [*I, too.*] Reminds me that
I might like to do a film column (books and movies of some interest to mystery readers), but I'm not sure that there is that
much appropriate stuff along the way. I don't need any more
commitments, and I've never sensed in you a deep and abiding
passion for movies. Would the readership be interested in reviews of French critical works? (I think Bleiler would, but
would anybody else?) They line up on my shelves, and once a
year I say a few kind words about them in my TAD bibliography.
    [*How about it, folks?*]

From Mike Nevins, 7045 Cornell, University City, MO 63130:
    Thanks for another excellent TMF, especially for Marv
Lachman's fascinating article about Rex Stout and the Presi-
dency, one of the best pieces you've ever published.

From Frank Floyd, Rt. 3, Box 139-F, Berryville, AR 72616:
    The little bundle of joy got here yesterday. Luckily, it
was wet and dreary yesterday here, and in the early afternoon
I was able to begin reading my *FANcier*. The letters that we
have had for the two issues preceding this last one have, like
David said, made my days. I am sure that everyone knows what

David--David D., of course. I wanted to taknk everyone who
tried to write something on my five suggested topics. Some of
the things they wrote were exceedingly interesting.

I bought a book the other day entitled *The Moving Target*.
It was written by John Macdonald, not John D. It is identical
to the book by the same name by Ross Macdonald. Alfred A
Knopf, Inc. first published this one in April, 1949. My copy
is a Pocket Book of March, 1950. [*Before settling on the Ross
Macdonald pseudonym, Kenneth Millar wrote as John Ross Macdonald, hence the confusion.*]

Our friend, and I mean the friend of all of us at the *FAN-
cier*, John McAleer, has a new book out called *Unit Pride*, I
understand. I hope he does as well on it as he did on his Rex
Stout biography.

The reason must be that there are times when I am crazy.
After reading the *FANcier* and seeing your announcement about
the Charles Scribner Crime Novel Award, I decided suddenly to
enter the contest. Working the long hours that I do and the
plodder that I am writing, there is no way that I am going to
get a novel written in the length of time between now and
September 30. All the same, I wrote an eleven page outline
last night, and now I am ready to write.

From Bob Sampson, 609 Holmes Ave., Huntsville, AL 35801:

Here's a brief piece, for your consideration, on one of
the numerous characters from *Detective Story Magazine*. [*See
"Peterman from the Old School" in this issue.*] I've done a
good deal of work on the series characters of the 1920's pulps,
looking at them as characters, first, and as examples, second,
of lines leading into present mystery fiction. Whether your
readers are interested in these obsolete old boys, I don't
know. If anybody has information about the author, Charles W.
Tyler, I'd appreciate hearing about it. My information is
confused.

From Bob Adey, 7 Highcroft Ave., Wordsley, Stourbridge, West
Midlands, DY8 5LX, England:

TMF vol. 5 #2 arrived recently and maintains its very good
form.

I was interested to read that Marvin Lachman's hard-boiled
favorites are the same as mine. He does, however, mention a
couple of authors, William Campbell Gault and Thomas B. Dewey,
I have never read. Are they indeed comparable to the witty
and amusing Browne and the thoughtful Ross Macdonald? Comments would be appreciated.

In an earlier letter I commented on Martin Wooster's criticism of *Twentieth Century Crime and Mystery Writers*, and,
after reading Bob Aucott's letter, I'd like to restate my
position--ever so slightly. The book is, in my opinion, a
most useful volume, but inevitably some of the essays err on
the academic side. I'm not going to pick out particular
essayists because, quite frankly, that would involve a lot of
rereading that I haven't at this point the time for. A few of
the essays also seemed to me to betray a certain lack of real
knowledge of the authors concerned. In fairness, they were in
the main the more obscure authors when perhaps it was a case
of half a loaf. All this is beginning (as I read it back) to
sound rather carping. It is not meant to be. It's simply
that with this kind of volume, a little of the overacademic

and the under researched is bound to come through. All things considered, Reilly should be preening himself.

As to the subject of the academic itself which has recently provoked interesting comment in your letter columns, I have to say that a certain kind of article/essay is entirely beyond my reading capability. I refer to the essay, almost always about a particular author or sub genre, which seeks to disect the author's books and draw all sorts of inferences from what he or she has written. They are frequently tied in with social comment and the point is that they simply "turn me off." A rather modern expression, but I can think of none more suitable. I'm sure that there are many readers who like these academic theses, but I don't happen to be one of them. They bore me to tears--or, to be strictly honest, they don't any more because I gave up trying to read them years ago. Now there may be others out there who don't like the sort of articles I like (for instance, bibliographical studies rarely fail to intrigue me), and that's fair enough as far as I'm concerned. The problem really ends up on the editor's desk, for he has the job, issue by issue, of trying to maintain a reasonable balance and keep all his readers happy. Most of the time they succeed, and, Guy, you and Jeff Meyerson have an almost unblemished record where this is concerned. TAD also avoided these pitfalls for many years, until it moved to its temporary West Coast faculty home. Then, I suspect, Al Hubin found himself suddenly inundated with articles of this kind (and by people of whom we'd never heard and from whom nothing more has been heard since), and this is why the percentage rose appreciably. Happily, the East Coast seems to agree with TAD rather more than the West. If I have this wrong, I'm sure Al will put me right.

Anyway, enough pontification for one letter.

I enclose cuttings from last week's *Radio Times* (which gives the non-commercial TV programmes as well) which gives details of a made-for-TV film (1975), apparently an unsuccessful pilot for a stillborn series. [*"Death Among Friends,"* starring Kate Reid and Martin Balsam.] I found it quite enjoyable and much better than some of those that went on for long runs. The lady detective, if unblievable, was nevertheless an interesting character, and the first murder was a good old fashioned impossible "footprints on the tennis court" plot with a different (and quite feasible) solution from that of Carr's *Problem of the Wire Cage*. So much more enjoyable than Vegas (very disappointing), Magnum, Charlie's Angels, Hart to Hart (what a waste of talent), which are our offerings from the U.S. Oh, for the return of Rockford, Harry O., Kojak. Talking of which, is anyone collecting those numerous TV spin-off books which now seem almost obligatory? I've started picking up a few of the British series spin offs and have been surprised at how many I have found--Public Eye (reviewed in TMF vol. 5, #2), The Expert, The Champions, The Avengers (three separate series), XYZ Man, The Mtrange Report, Danger Man, Honey West, The Ratcatchers, Sapphire and Steel, Jason King, The Professionals, Dixon of Dock Green, The Enigma Files, Shoestring, Softly, Softly, Z Cars, Sergeant Cork, Raffles, The Sandbaggers--and some of them will be the rarities of the future.

Finally, Jon and Rita Breen have explained my Holmes reference to perfection. That's exactly what I meant. [*Re*

the block question--I just finished rereading Dick Francis'
second book, Nerve *(I should have said, second novel), in*
which a character says there is a certain business "two roads
over." This was in London. An American would surely have
said "two blocks over," or "two blocks away." Nerve, *by the*
way, is a marvelous thriller.]

From Mike Cook, 3318 Wimberg Ave., Evansville, IN 47712:
    Just a note to advise that *Monthly Murders* is now com-
plete and in the hands of the publisher, Greenwood Press. On
the digest-size U.S. and British mystery magazines, it will
be 1,141 pages plus introductory pages, and will include a
chronological listing of all the fiction, and then an authors'
composite listing of over 31,000 stories.
    And I'm knee-deep into my next book, to be titled *Fan Fare,*
a composite, cross-referenced index (including all book reviews and letters) for forty fan and semi-professional magazines in the fields of: Mystery & Detective (21 magazines),
Pulps (11 magazines), Dime Novels (2 magazines), Boys' Book
collecting (4 magazines), and Paperback collecting (2 magazines). It appears it will be near 1,000 pages.

www.ingramcontent.com/pod-product-compliance
Lightning Source LLC
Chambersburg PA
CBHW031616040426
42452CB00006B/542

* 9 7 8 1 4 3 4 4 3 6 2 6 9 *